Getting the Train

The History of Scotland's Railways

David Ross

Polmadie Locomotive shed, Glasgow, 1938. (Stenlake Collection)

Stenlake Publishing Ltd.

For Fynn and Sandy, and their friends

Books on Scottish Railway History by David Ross

The Highland Railway (2010)
The Caledonian: Scotland's Imperial Railway (2013)
The North British Railway: A History (2014)
The Glasgow & SouthWestern Railway: A History (2014)
The Great North of Scotland Railway: A New History (2015)
Scottish Railways 1923-2016: A History (2017)

© 2017 David Ross
First Published in the United Kingdom, 2017
Stenlake Publishing Limited
54-58 Mill Square, Catrine, KA5 6RD
01290 551122
www.stenlake.co.uk
ISBN 978 1 84033 771 6

Printed by
Berforts, 17 Burgess Road, TN35 4NR

CONTENTS

Foreword   4

Maps   5

1. The First Lines – 1812-1845   11

2. The Mania and After – 1845-1850   15

3. Competition and Expansion – the 1850s   22

4. Consolidation and Combination – the 1860s   26

5. Maturity Sets in – the 1870s   33

6. Public Service or Private Profit? – the 1880s   38

7. Last Years of the Monopoly Era – the 1890s   47

8. Modernise or Economise? – 1900-1914   55

9. World War I and the Grouping – 1914-1922   61

10. The Big Two – 1923-1939   67

11. World War II and Nationalisation – 1939-1959   76

12. A Decade of Radical Change – 1960-1969   87

13. The Gradual Reinvention of British Railways

    – the 1970s and 80s   92

14. A Privatised Railway – 1990-2016   100

FOREWORD

Scotland came into the modern world on railway tracks. Each time you step on a train you extend the continuity of a colourful strand in the national story. Once wreathed in steam, now with pristine electric and diesel trains, Scottish railways reach two hundred years into the past and point to the future. The people of Scotland might well take a keen interest in their railways. They currently pay a total subsidy of over £700 million a year to a subsidiary of the state-owned Netherlands Railways for operation of their passenger trains, and Network Rail (owned by the British Government), for maintenance of tracks, signalling and stations. That's £140 for every man, woman and child in the country. The way in which Scotland's and Britain's railway system is financed and run has generated fierce argument almost from the start and continues to do so today.

Getting the train can simply mean to step on board in order to go somewhere. Or it can have the wider sense of 'understanding'. To get the train in that way is to know how the railway system was set up, how it works, and what it is for. All these senses apply in this book. Away from its public face, the real, almost secret, life of the railway rests, as always, on weights and measures. How much power to get a 1,000-tonne freight train over Beattock at a speed which will not hold up the Pendolinos? How to squeeze modern containers along track built to tight clearances in the 1850s? Around these basics a story forms: how the railways began, and grew, and played their part in the formation of present-day Scotland. It explains how they were perceived by the owners and managers, by workers, by users, and by government. These points of view, often inconsistent and always changeable, supplied the context in which the railways worked, and still do today. Inevitably, an increasingly political dimension appears, especially from 1958 onwards, when governments were forced to address the massive financial implications of a modern railway system. In recounting the story, examples from every period shed light on the general trend of events. Hundreds of millions of pounds were invested, many thousands of people were involved – there can hardly be a family in the country that does not have some ancestral or historic link with the railways.

This is the first full history of Scottish railways to be published. It's the book I would like to have had when I first became interested in the subject, and I hope that others will find it a useful introduction to all that lies behind the simple action of getting the train. Interested readers can explore the subject further in the six books listed on page 2, which are fully referenced and annotated.

Note on money: All sums are quoted in the value of their time. Money values were fairly stable until 1914, when the purchasing power of the pound sterling began to decline, and wages rose. Untill then, most railway workers earned around £1 a week. A driver in 1913 earned around £60 a year for a week of up to 60 hours; in 2015 ScotRail drivers earned £43,212 a year for a 35-hour week. Sterling was denominated in pounds, shillings and pence (£,s,d) until the introduction of decimal coinage in 1971.

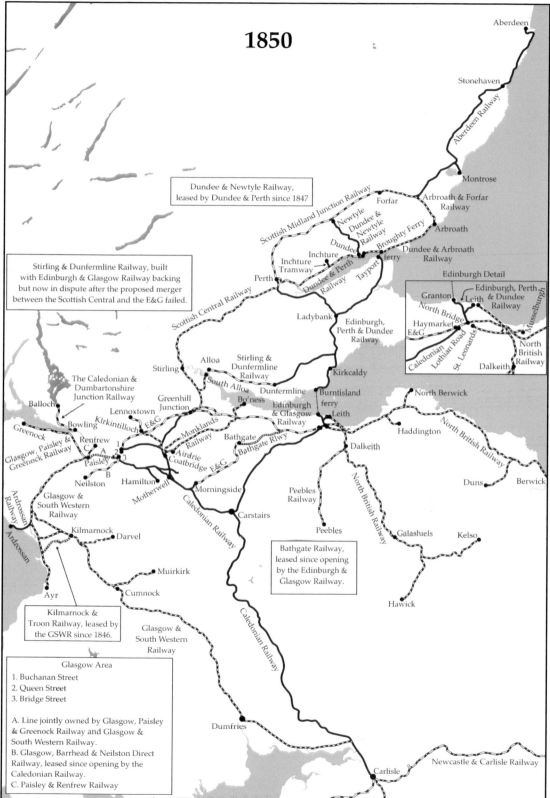

1850

Aberdeen

Stonehaven

Aberdeen Railway

Montrose

Arbroath & Forfar Railway

Forfar

Arbroath

Dundee & Arbroath Railway

Dundee & Newtyle Railway, leased by Dundee & Perth since 1847

Scottish Midland Junction Railway

Newtyle

Dundee & Newtyle Railway

Dundee

Broughty Ferry

ferry

Inchture

Inchture Tramway

Dundee & Perth Railway

Tayport

Perth

Stirling & Dunfermline Railway, built with Edinburgh & Glasgow Railway backing but now in dispute after the proposed merger between the Scottish Central and the E&G failed.

Scottish Central Railway

Ladybank

Edinburgh, Perth & Dundee Railway

Edinburgh Detail

Granton

North Bridge

Leith

Edinburgh, Perth & Dundee Railway

Musselburgh

Haymarket
E&G

Caledonian

Lothian Road

St. Leonards

North British Railway

Dalkeith

Alloa

Stirling & Dunfermline Railway

Kirkcaldy

South Alloa

The Caledonian & Dumbartonshire Junction Railway

Stirling

Greenhill Junction

Bo'ness

Dunfermline

Burntisland ferry

North Berwick

Balloch

Lennoxtown

E&G

Kirkintilloch

Monklands Railway

Bathgate

Edinburgh & Glasgow Railway

Leith

Haddington

North British Railway

Bowling

Greenock

Glasgow, Paisley & Greenock Railway

Renfrew

C A
1
2
3
B

Paisley

Airdrie

Coatbridge E&G

Bathgate Rlwy

Dalkeith

Neilston

Hamilton

Motherwell

Morningside

Peebles Railway

Duns

Berwick

Ardrossan Railway

Glasgow & South Western Railway

Kilmarnock

Darvel

Caledonian Railway

Carstairs

Peebles

North British Railway

Galashiels

Kelso

Ardrossan

Bathgate Railway, leased since opening by the Edinburgh & Glasgow Railway.

Muirkirk

Ayr

Cumnock

Kilmarnock & Troon Railway, leased by the GSWR since 1846.

Glasgow & South Western Railway

Hawick

Caledonian Railway

Dumfries

Glasgow Area

1. Buchanan Street
2. Queen Street
3. Bridge Street

A. Line jointly owned by Glasgow, Paisley & Greenock Railway and Glasgow & South Western Railway.
B. Glasgow, Barrhead & Neilston Direct Railway, leased since opening by the Caledonian Railway.
C. Paisley & Renfrew Railway

Carlisle

Newcastle & Carlisle Railway

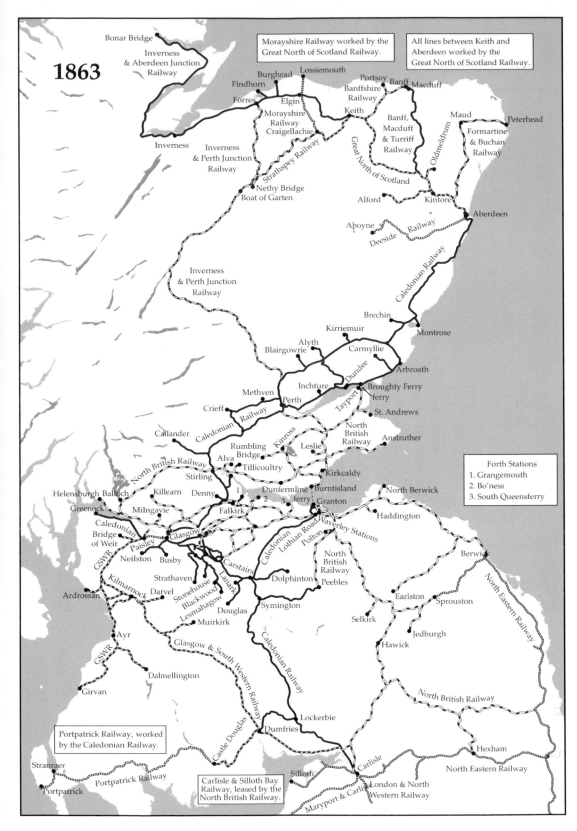

1863

Bonar Bridge

Inverness & Aberdeen Junction Railway

Morayshire Railway worked by the Great North of Scotland Railway.

All lines between Keith and Aberdeen worked by the Great North of Scotland Railway.

Lossiemouth
Burghead
Findhorn
Portsoy Banff Macduff
Banffshire Railway
Forres Elgin Keith
Inverness
Morayshire Railway Craigellachie
Maud
Banff, Macduff & Turriff Railway
Oldmeldrum
Peterhead
Formartine & Buchan Railway

Inverness & Perth Junction Railway
Strathspey Railway
Great North of Scotland
Nethy Bridge
Boat of Garten

Alford
Kintore
Aberdeen

Apoyne
Deeside Railway

Inverness & Perth Junction Railway

Caledonian Railway

Brechin
Montrose
Kirriemuir
Alyth
Blairgowrie
Carmyllie

Dundee
Arbroath

Methven
Inchture
Crieff
Perth
Broughty Ferry ferry
Tayport
St. Andrews

Callander
Caledonian Railway

Rumbling Bridge
Kinross
Leslie
North British Railway
Anstruther

Alva
Tillicoultry
Stirling
Kirkcaldy

Killearn
Denny
Dunfermline ferry
Burntisland
North Berwick

Forth Stations
1. Grangemouth
2. Bo'ness
3. South Queensferry

Helensburgh Balloch
1
2   3
Granton
Haddington

Greenock
Milngavie
Falkirk

Caledonian Bridge of Weir
Glasgow
Lothian Road
Waverley Stations
Polton

Paisley
Carstairs
North British Railway
Berwick

GSWR
Neilston
Busby
Lanark
Dolphinton
Peebles

Strathaven
Dolphinton
Earlston
Sprouston

Ardrossan
Kilmarnock
Darvel
Stonehouse
Blackwood
Lesmahagow
Symington
Selkirk
Jedburgh

Ayr
Muirkirk
Douglas
Hawick

GSWR
Glasgow & South Western Railway

Dalmellington
Girvan

Caledonian Railway

Portpatrick Railway, worked by the Caledonian Railway.

Lockerbie
Dumfries
Castle Douglas

Hexham

Stranraer
Portpatrick Railway
Silloth
Carlisle
North Eastern Railway

Portpatrick

Carlisle & Silloth Bay Railway, leased by the North British Railway.

Maryport & Carlisle
London & North Western Railway

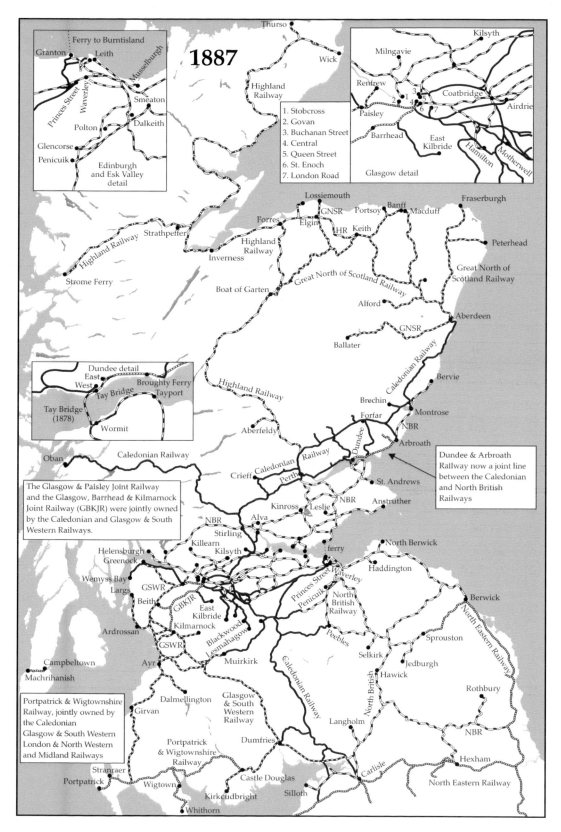

1887

Ferry to Burntisland
Granton
Leith
Musselburgh
Waverley
Princes Street
Smeaton
Polton
Dalkeith
Glencorse
Penicuik
Edinburgh
and Esk Valley
detail

1. Stobcross
2. Govan
3. Buchanan Street
4. Central
5. Queen Street
6. St. Enoch
7. London Road

Kilsyth
Milngavie
Renfrew
Coatbridge
Paisley
Airdrie
Barrhead
East Kilbride
Hamilton
Motherwell

Glasgow detail

Thurso
Wick
Highland Railway

Lossiemouth
GNSR
Portsoy
Banff
Macduff
Fraserburgh
Forres
Elgin
HR
Keith
Peterhead
Strathpeffer
Highland Railway
Inverness
Great North of Scotland Railway
Great North of Scotland Railway
Strome Ferry
Boat of Garten
Alford
Aberdeen
Ballater
GNSR

Dundee detail
East
West
Broughty Ferry
Tay Bridge
Tayport
Tay Bridge (1878)
Wormit

Caledonian Railway
Highland Railway
Bervie
Brechin
Forfar
Montrose
Aberfeldy
NBR
Dundee
Arbroath

Oban
Caledonian Railway
Crieff
Caledonian Railway
Perth
St. Andrews
Dundee & Arbroath Railway now a joint line between the Caledonian and North British Railways

The Glasgow & Paisley Joint Railway and the Glasgow, Barrhead & Kilmarnock Joint Railway (GBKJR) were jointly owned by the Caledonian and Glasgow & South Western Railways.

Kinross
Leslie
NBR
Anstruther
Alva
Stirling
NBR
Killearn
Kilsyth
North Berwick
ferry
Haddington
Helensburgh
Greenock
Princes Street
Waverley
Wemyss Bay
Largs
GSWR
North British Railway
Berwick
Beith
GBKJR
East Kilbride
Kilmarnock
Blackwood
Lesmahagow
Peebles
Sprouston
North Eastern Railway
Ardrossan
GSWR
Muirkirk
Selkirk
Jedburgh
Campbeltown
Ayr
Hawick
Machrihanish
Dalmellington
Glasgow & South Western Railway
Rothbury

Portpatrick & Wigtownshire Railway, jointly owned by the Caledonian Glasgow & South Western London & North Western and Midland Railways

Girvan
Caledonian Railway
North British Railway
Langholm
NBR
Dumfries
Hexham
Portpatrick & Wigtownshire Railway
Stranraer
Carlisle
North Eastern Railway
Portpatrick
Wigtown
Castle Douglas
Silloth
Kirkcudbright
Whithorn

7

1923 LMS and LNER Networks

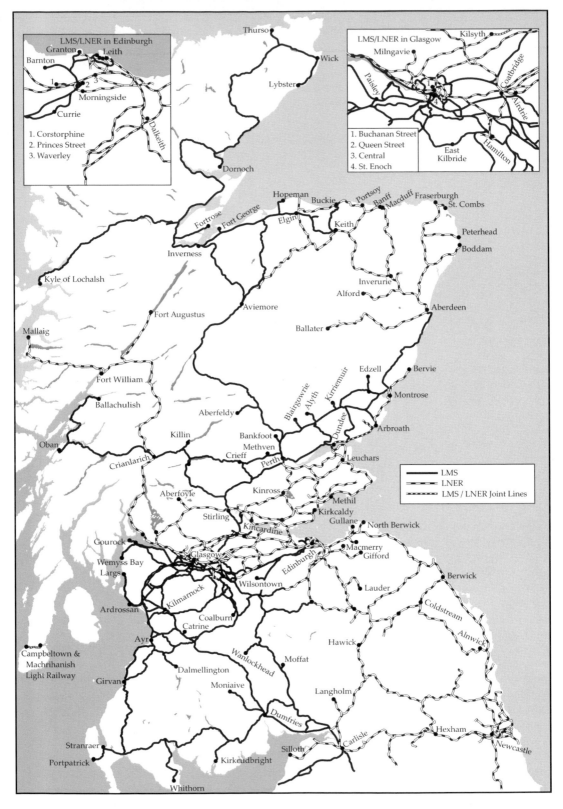

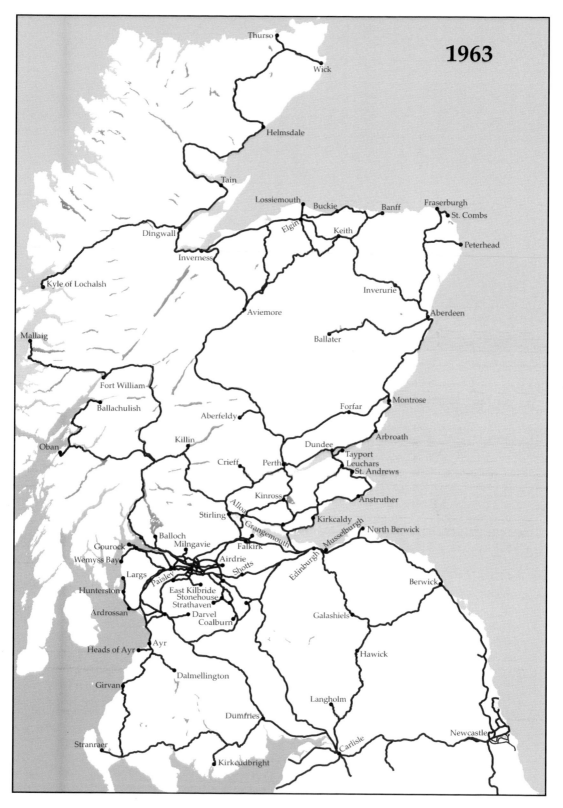

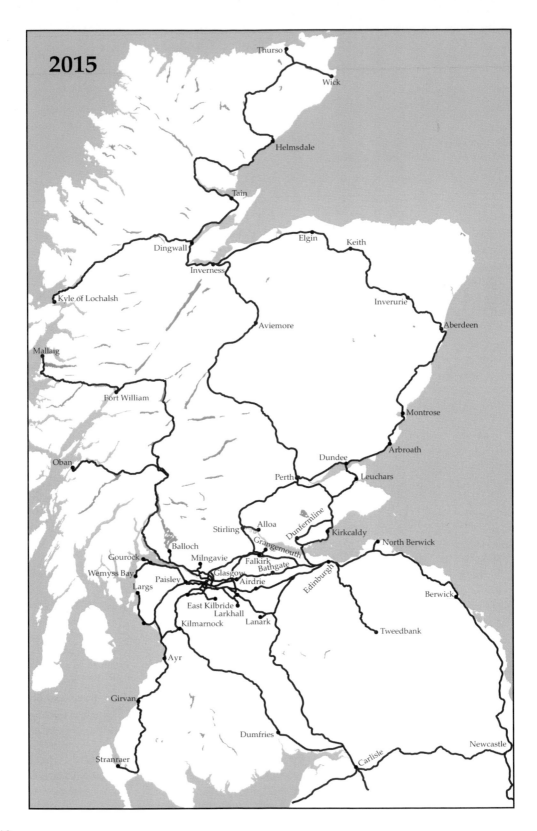

2015

Thurso
Wick
Helmsdale
Tain
Dingwall
Elgin
Keith
Inverness
Kyle of Lochalsh
Inverurie
Aviemore
Aberdeen
Mallaig
Fort William
Montrose
Oban
Arbroath
Dundee
Perth
Leuchars
Alloa
Stirling
Dunfermline
Kirkcaldy
Balloch
Grangemouth
North Berwick
Gourock
Milngavie
Falkirk
Wemyss Bay
Paisley
Glasgow
Bathgate
Larkhall
Airdrie
Edinburgh
Largs
Berwick
East Kilbride
Larkhall
Kilmarnock
Lanark
Tweedbank
Ayr
Girvan
Dumfries
Newcastle
Stranraer
Carlisle

The First Lines – 1812-1845

From Wagonway to Railway

The start of railways lies with the mining industry. Benefiting from early technical books published in Central Europe, and personal contacts in what was already an international network of mining technicians, in the 17th century Scottish collieries began to run wheeled wagons downhill on wooden rails from the pit-heads, carrying house coal to waiting ships at a nearby harbour. Ponies would haul the empty wagons up again. Wagonways existed in coal districts along the north and south shores of the Firth of Forth and the Ayrshire coast, part of the technics of mining, and no-one seems to have thought of any wider application for them. Over longer distances, canals became the accepted mode of bulk transport during the 18th century. In 1793 the Marquess of Titchfield, or his advisers, changed their minds about digging a 10-mile canal between his coal pits at Kilmarnock and a new harbour at a promontory called The Troon, and decided instead to make a wagonway. To help defray their costs the proprietors established Scotland's first public railway, opened on 6 July 1812, and available for use, at a charge, by anyone who had a vehicle to fit the rails. These were L-shaped, so a flat-wheeled cart could easily go from road to rail so long as it fitted the line's 4ft 4in (1.32m) gauge.

The Kilmarnock & Troon Railway was a success, with a range of traffic including a passenger carriage known as the 'Fair Trader'. In 1817 it experimented with the first steam locomotive to run in Scotland, supplied by George Stephenson from Killingworth in Northumberland, but the engine's weight broke the short, brittle rail sections and it was quickly sold on. The steam locomotive's great days had not yet come, though dedicated men in various places were working to improve it – one of

This 1820s painting by an unknown artist shows the Kilmarnock & Troon Railway, with the 'Fair Trader' coach passing a coal train. (East Ayrshire Council)

them, Timothy Burstall, would send an engine from Edinburgh to the Rainhill trials in 1829 where Stephenson's *Rocket* eclipsed all other contenders. By the mid-1830s, engines and rails had become far more reliable, and horse traction was used only for short distances. In the mining area east of Glasgow, new railways were at work, beginning with the Monkland & Kirkintilloch, opened in 1826. Coal haulage was the main purpose, though it was also found that large numbers of people wanted to travel on them. The same happened with the Edinburgh & Dalkeith Railway (1831). One of the first railways to carry only general goods (and passengers) was the line from Dundee to Newtyle, crossing the Sidlaw Hills in 1831 by tunnels and steep gradients to link Dundee's port and mills with the flax-growing farmlands of Strathmore.

For fifteen or so years before that, the idea of a national network of railways throughout Great Britain had been discussed. One of those who drew lines on maps was Robert Stevenson, of the Edinburgh engineering and poetry family, who surveyed a line through Strathmore to Aberdeen in the early 1820s, and calculated that railways could reduce the number of draught horses in Scotland from 60,000 to 10,000. By 1835 some shrewd and wealthy merchants and businessmen realised that civil and mechanical engineering could cope with large-scale railway building and operation, and their London & Birmingham Railway, opened in 1838, was seen as the first stage of a railway that would extend to Edinburgh and Glasgow. Across Britain, surveys were being made for new lines, and local committees were being formed to organise finance and get the necessary permissions. In 1837 Scotland's first main line, from Glasgow to Ayr, was authorised by an Act of Parliament and on 12 August 1840 the Glasgow, Paisley, Kilmarnock & Ayr Railway (GPKAR, known as 'the Ayrshire') opened from a station at Bridge Street, Glasgow, to a terminus at Newton-on-Ayr. It had a branch to Ardrossan. By taking a train to Ardrossan, then the fast steamer *Fire King* to Liverpool, and a train from Liverpool to London, it was possible for the first time to travel between Glasgow and London inside 24 hours. In 1840 this was amazing, but within five years would seem absurdly long. Close

A contemporary depiction of the opening of Ayr Station on 12 August 1840. (Hutton Collection)

behind was the Edinburgh & Glasgow Railway, which opened between termini at Haymarket in Edinburgh and Queen Street in Glasgow on 21 February 1842, using up-to-the-minute steam locomotives to move goods and passengers between the cities at the astounding speed of 40 miles an hour. Its promoters raised capital of £999,000 to finance it, and it proved comfortably profitable, paying dividends of 5% or more a year to its investors.

Over the Border

In both Glasgow and Edinburgh action was going ahead for lines that would run southwards to join up with railways being built in England. Rivalry arose here, as the economists of the day were convinced that there was only enough potential traffic for one Scottish-English railway link. Would it be from Edinburgh via Berwick and Newcastle, or from Glasgow via Carlisle? And if the latter, should the line go by Dumfries and Kilmarnock, or by Lockerbie and Carstairs? In 1841 a Government inquiry reported in favour of a line coming up through western England to Carlisle and continuing past Lockerbie and Beattock to Glasgow, with a branch to Edinburgh. This was good news for its promoters, who had decided to call their line the Caledonian Railway. A Glasgow committee had been formed to support the line via Dumfries and they did not give up. They were already running the 'Ayrshire' and considered it the natural northern section of the Anglo-Scottish route.

Whatever the economists might say, it soon became clear that there would be more than one railway into England. In Edinburgh, the dynamic John Learmonth, an ex-Lord Provost and joint chairman of the Edinburgh & Glasgow Railway, concerned to keep his city at the leading edge of railway development, gained Parliamentary approval in 1844 for a line from Edinburgh to Berwick on Tweed. Its ambition to be the country's premier line was clear in its name, the North British Railway, and its promoters were in touch with George Hudson of York, England's 'Railway King', to create the 'East Coast' route to London, which they hoped would beat the 'West Coast' to completion.

Looking northwards, the concept of a Stirling-Perth-Aberdeen line, linked to the line from England and to the Edinburgh & Glasgow Railway, had been promoted since the mid-1830s. By 1844 several separate companies were proposing to share the task. From a junction at Greenhill, the Scottish Central Railway was to run to Perth. From there the Scottish Midland Junction Railway would continue to Forfar, and the Aberdeen Railway would form the final part. Beyond Aberdeen, the Great North of Scotland Railway proposed to build onwards to Inverness. Already, though, there was inter-company hostility and dissension. The Edinburgh & Glasgow company was opposed to the Caledonian project, which would divide at Carstairs with a line to each city. A short link at the junction would make two competing railways between the two main centres of population.

The Railway Promoters

Most of the railway promoters of the 1830s were rich men. Sometimes their wealth had unexpected sources. James McCall, first chairman of the Ayrshire company, had done well out of the £20,000,000 payout from the British Government to the owners of slaves in sugar plantations: he was not a direct owner but had lent a large sum to one estate and had a prior claim on its share of the loot. Twenty years later, Alexander Matheson, chairman of the companies that ultimately formed the Highland Railway, directed some of his fortune from the Hong Kong opium trade (officially approved) on the construction of the first railways from Inverness. McCall had been a wine merchant, John Learmonth and John Leadbetter, joint chairmen of the Edinburgh & Glasgow Railway, were respectively the owner of a coach-building works and a linen merchant. Another early chairman, John James Hope-Johnstone, might have passed his life as a Dumfries-shire country landowner if he had not seen the usefulness of the Caledonian Railway to bring coal and lime to his Annandale estates, and accepted the role of its first chairman.

The chairmen had to show vision and energy. They had no map, no-one's footsteps to follow: it was their experience – and their undoing – to find that things did not stop with the making and operating of a railway from town A to town B. Railway companies seemed to have an inbuilt urge to throw out branch lines, to build into empty territory or to invade that of other companies in order to steal their traffic and revenues, while at the same time making strenuous efforts to prevent others from doing the same unto them. As expansion and competition grew, the backers of railway schemes found that they had embarked on a hugely expensive exercise. Surveyors had to be hired, lawyers had to be briefed, Parliamentary counsel had to be employed to steer each Bill through the process of examination before the railway got its Act; then land had to be bought, engineers had to design every detail, labourers had to be hired, rails purchased, bridges, stations and tunnels had to be built, engines and rolling stock had to be acquired, permanent staff had to be recruited. Already this required very large amounts of capital, but three factors pushed it up to an almost intolerable extent. First of all, people with specialist knowledge of engineering and railway planning were in very short supply and commanded huge fees. Secondly, landowners quickly saw the railways as a bonanza, demanding high prices for often unproductive ground and extravagant compensation for the loss of their 'amenities'. A railway's Act of Parliament gave it power of compulsory land purchase but did not control the price. Thirdly, as already noted, railway companies, or committees set up to promote new railways, spent enormous sums in opposing the plans of competitors. In 1844 the Edinburgh & Glasgow, the newly-formed North British, the Ayrshire, and the committee of the proposed Glasgow, Dumfries & Carlisle Railway spent £30,000 – a sum equivalent to over £1,500,000 today – of capital supposedly raised to build their own lines to oppose the passing of the Caledonian Railway Bill. The Caledonian got its Act, however, and immediately proposed an east-west Caledonian Extension Railway, deliberately intended to take traffic away from these 'enemy' companies. That plan failed, but from the 1840s to the 1890s, the cost to the Scottish railways of opposing one another's plans, and mounting counter-plans, would run into many millions of pounds: many hundreds of millions in current money.

In railway promotion the key people were lawyers, with bankers close behind. Solicitors were important in local networks, dealing with businessmen, landowners and rich farmers: people who believed in progress through commerce and industry, often themselves entrepreneurial, ambitious and keen to become rich, or richer. Landowning families frequently had younger sons established as local bank agents or writers (as solicitors were known). Banks were already well-established in economic life: at the end of 1837 there were 24 banking companies with 274 offices, and new ones being set up, all happy to lend funds for railway construction. With the excitement of potential financial gains running through these district networks, the formation of railway companies went ahead briskly. The new trade of stock-broking arose from dealings in railway shares, and stock exchanges were opened in Glasgow and Edinburgh by 1846, later also in Aberdeen and Dundee. Many investors in Scottish main lines – 80% in the Caledonian's case – were from England, keen to share in the rewards of a growing British national system. George Hudson invested £21,250 in the North British at a moment when it was dangerously short of funds.

The Mania and After – 1845-50

The Transport Revolution

In the 1840s it was clear to everyone that a transport revolution was under way. One point in particular was established – steam-powered trains did not simply take over the existing traffic along their route, but generated additional custom on a large scale. Farmers, coal mines, manufacturers and merchants of all kinds had a widened range for business, at a cheaper rate per mile. And for the first time, large numbers of people could travel long distances over land at exciting and previously impossible speeds. Everyone's horizons were being widened.

Roads were seen as common property under the Crown, with main highways in the care of turnpike trusts, which charged tolls for maintenance but were non-profit bodies. Public railways, though, began and continued as capitalist ventures to make profits for investors. The early multi-user idea could not survive the advent of the locomotive, which made it essential for the traffic to be concentrated into trainloads and properly managed in the interest of efficiency and safety. No small or occasional user was going to invest in a steam locomotive. The owning company either had to provide the motive power and the operating system, or rent its line to someone else who would do so. At this time, political and public opinion were very much against monopoly of any trade or service, but also against government interfering with private business or dictating what form it should take. Railways produced a new situation, which had politicians flummoxed. Some parliamentarians took refuge in the idea that railway companies would duplicate one another's lines, so ensuring competition and keeping down rates and charges. To the more far-sighted, it was obvious that the huge cost of setting up a railway would prevent such competition on all but the most lucrative of routes; and equally obvious that in the long run, railway companies were more likely to amalgamate with each other than to compete head-on, so making an even greater monopoly.

The most influential economic writer of the time, the Scot John Ramsay McCulloch, author of *Principles of Political Economy*, thought government interference was only acceptable in the area of public utilities – when a company had exclusive privileges, its dividends and charges should be subject to limitation. McCulloch certainly saw railways in this light, and his view that the government should take powers to control them influenced William Ewart Gladstone, about to become President of the Board of Trade in Peel's Tory government of 1844. Gladstone was one

Lord Dalhousie (1812-60), the man who might have master-minded a planned railway system.

of very few politicians to face up to the new transport phenomenon. He proposed legislation that would go a long way towards state control, including giving the government the right to buy up railways under certain conditions. Two men with Scottish connections were his allies. One was James Morrison, "the richest commoner in Britain", a man of radical ideas despite his huge wealth. The son of a Hampshire publican of Scottish descent, he was Liberal MP for Inverness Burghs from 1841 to 1847. The other was a Scottish peer, James Ramsay, Lord Dalhousie. Morrison succeeded in having a specialist body, led by Dalhousie, set up to supervise railway matters, but it lasted less than a year. Dalhousie's biographer wrote that had he been allowed a free hand, he "would have from the first secured for the public an effective control by the State over railway extension, and would have treated the new system of communication as a matter of national concern." Gladstone's Railway Bill was very much watered down in the face of massive opposition from the railway companies, though the resulting Regulation of Railways Act (1844) included one important and long-lasting clause:

> … that each Company be required to run over their line on each weekday at least one train conveying third class passengers in carriages provided with seats and protected from the weather, at a speed of not less than twelve miles an hour, including stoppages, and at a fare not exceeding one penny a mile for adults, children under twelve half-price, and under three free, 56lb of luggage to be allowed without charge.

Since 1842 the companies had had to pay a passenger tax of 5% of the fare charged (formerly levied on stage coaches), which meant reporting their passenger numbers and receipts. 'Parliamentary' trains were exempted from the passenger duty. The need for specifying closed carriages shows how the railways had been treating third class passengers till then: open wagons without roofs or seats were normal. On the new Paisley-Greenock line a local minister was seen among those standing in a third class wagon. Chaffed about this by a friend, he replied, "Where else would you find me but among the congregation of the upright?". Parliamentary trains were grudgingly run, often at unsocial hours, and companies still concentrated their attention on the first and second class passengers. Third class cost slightly more than Parliamentary, but even so, many trains had no third class accommodation.

The great majority of people had neither the funds nor the interest to buy railway shares, but they accepted the steam railway with remarkable ease. After all, steam power in fixed engines had been operating in textile mills and at pit-heads for decades. Speed was the great novelty, and the public quickly got used to it, becoming critical of delays and slow services, especially on the Parliamentary trains and those that included third class carriages. In the 19th century more than three quarters of Scottish railway journeys were made in third class, compared to just under 58% in England. When it got going in 1852, the Great North company, uniquely among British railways, spared itself the expense of building second class carriages: first and third were the only options.

Following the government's failure in 1844-45 to take decisive action, Parliament did little more than sit on the sidelines for forty years watching company scrimmages. Its role was confined to approving or refusing new lines, with no reference to any overall plan; to ensuring through the Board of Trade's railway department that all companies conformed to certain basic safety regulations; and allowing or refusing alterations in the founding Acts which defined the companies' powers. At different times, it looked favourably on company amalgamations or refused them on principle. As an increasingly vital basic utility, but run by independent companies whose prime concern was to earn dividends for their shareholders, railways remained an

KILMARNOCK & TROON RAILWAY.

LIST OF TOLLS

Authorised by the KILMARNOCK & TROON RAILWAY ACT, 1846,

AND WHICH WILL BE EXACTED BY

THE GLASGOW & SOUTH WESTERN RAILWAY COMPANY,

Upon the said KILMARNOCK & TROON RAILWAY.

I:—ON THE USE OF THE SAID RAILWAY.

IN RESPECT OF THE TONNAGE OF ALL ARTICLES

Conveyed upon the said KILMARNOCK & TROON RAILWAY, or any part thereof, as follows:—

For all Dung, Compost, and all sorts of Manure, and Culm, per Ton per Mile, *One Penny*; and if conveyed by Carriages belonging to the Company, an additional sum, per Ton per Mile, of *One Halfpenny.*

For all Coal, Lime, and Limestone, and all Undressed Materials for the Repair of Public Roads or Highways, per Ton per Mile, *One Penny Halfpenny*; and if conveyed by Carriages belonging to the Company, an additional sum, per Ton per Mile, of *One Halfpenny.*

For all Coke, Charcoal, and Cinders; all Stones for Building, Pitching, and Paving; all Bricks, Tiles, Slates, Clay, Sand, and Ironstone, and Iron Ore, Pig-Iron, Bar-Iron, Rod-Iron, Hoop-Iron, and all other similar descriptions of Wrought Iron, and Iron Castings, not Manufactured into Utensils or other Articles of Merchandise, per Ton per Mile, *Twopence Halfpenny*; and if conveyed in Carriages belonging to the Company, an additional sum, per Ton per Mile, of *One Penny.*

For all Sugar, Grain, Corn, Flour, Hides, Dyewoods, Earthenware, Timber, Staves, and Deals, Metals (except Iron), Nails, Anvils, Vices, and Chains, per Ton per Mile, *Twopence*; and if conveyed in

Carriages belonging to the Company, an additional sum, per Ton per Mile, of *One Penny Halfpenny*

For all Cotton and other Wools, Drugs, Manufactured Goods, and all other Wares, Merchandise, Fish, Articles, Matters, or things, per Ton per Mile, *Threepence*; and if conveyed in Carriages belonging to the Company, an additional sum, per Ton per Mile, of *One Penny.*

For every Carriage, of whatever Description, not being a Carriage adapted and used for Travelling on a Railway, and not Weighing more than One Ton, carried or conveyed on a Truck or Platform, per Mile, *Sixpence*; and a like sum of *Sixpence* per Mile, for every additional Quarter of a Ton, or Fractional part of a Quarter of a Ton, which any such Carriage may weigh; and if conveyed on a Truck or Platform belonging to the Company, an additional sum, per Mile, of *Sixpence.*

For every Locomotive Engine without a Load, that is not drawing or propelling a Train of Loaded Carriages or Waggons, per Mile, *Ninepence.*

For every Railway Carriage or Waggon without a Load, per Mile, *One Halfpenny.*

EXEMPTIONS FROM THE PRECEDING TOLLS.

1. Locomotive Engines without a Load, or Railway Carriages or Waggons without a Load, going to fetch a Load, and returning therewith along the portion of the Railway over which such Engines or Carriages or Waggons have passed without such Load, are exempt from the above Tolls on such portion.

2. Locomotive Engines without a Load, or Railway Carriages or Waggons without a Load, on their return journey along the portion of the Railway over which such Engines and Carriages or Waggons have passed with a Load, are exempt from the above Tolls on such portion; provided always that this last exemption shall not be available, in respect of any Load, when any benefit under the first exemption has been claimed in respect of the same Load.

IN RESPECT OF PASSENGERS AND ANIMALS

Conveyed in Carriages upon the said KILMARNOCK & TROON RAILWAY, as follows:—

For any Person conveyed in or upon any such Carriage, per Mile, *Twopence*; and if conveyed in or upon any Carriage belonging to the Company, an additional sum of *One Penny.*

For every Horse, Mule, Ass, or other Beast of Draught or Burden, and for every Ox, Cow, Bull, or Neat Cattle, conveyed in or upon any Carriage, per Mile, *Twopence*; and if conveyed in or

upon any Carriage belonging to the Company, an additional sum of *Threepence.*

For every Calf, Pig, Sheep, Lamb, or other small Animal, conveyed in or upon any such Carriage, per Mile, *One Penny*; and if conveyed in or upon any Carriage belonging to the Company, an additional sum of *One Penny Halfpenny.*

II:—FOR THE USE OF ENGINES FOR PROPELLING CARRIAGES ON THE SAID RAILWAY,

One Penny per Mile for each Passenger or Animal, or for each Ton of Goods or other Articles, in addition to the above Tolls.

PROVISIONS AND REGULATIONS

APPLICABLE TO THE FIXING OF THE FORESAID TOLLS:—

For Articles conveyed, on the said Kilmarnock & Troon Railway, for a less Distance than Six Miles, the Company will demand Tolls as for Six entire Miles; and in addition to the prescribed Tolls for Conveyance, a reasonable charge for the Expense of Stopping, Loading, and Unloading.

For a Fraction of a Mile beyond Six Miles, or beyond any greater number of Miles, the Company will demand Tolls on Merchandise for such Fraction in proportion to the number of Quarters of a Mile; and if there be a Fraction of a Quarter of a Mile, such Fraction shall be deemed a Quarter of a Mile; and in respect of Passengers, every Fraction of a Mile beyond an integral number of Miles shall be deemed a Mile.

For a Fraction of a Ton the Company will demand Toll according to the number of Quarters of a Ton in such Fraction; and if there be a Fraction of a Quarter of a Ton, such Fraction shall be deemed a Quarter of a Ton.

With respect to all Articles except Stone or Timber, the Weight shall be determined according to the usual Avoirdupois Weight.

With respect to Stone and Timber, Fourteen Cubic Feet of Stone, Forty Cubic Feet of Oak, Mahogany, Teak, Beach or Ash, and Fifty Cubic Feet of any other Timber, shall be deemed One Ton Weight; and so in proportion, for any smaller Quantity.

And with respect to Small Packages, and Single Articles of great Weight, notwithstanding the Rate of Toll above prescribed, the Company will demand the Tolls following:—

For the Carriage of Small Parcels, that is to say, Parcels not exceeding Five Hundred Pounds Weight each:—

1st—For every Parcel not exceeding 56 Lbs. carried a distance not exceeding 10 Miles, *One Shilling and Sixpence*, and for any additional distance, *One Halfpenny* per Mile.

2d—For every Parcel exceeding 56 Lbs. and not exceeding 500 Lbs. carried a distance not exceeding 10 Miles, *Six Shillings*, and for any additional distance, *Twopence Halfpenny* per Mile. Provided always that Articles sent in large aggregate quantities, although made up

of separate Parcels, such as Bags of Sugar, Coffee, Meal, and the like, shall not be deemed Small Parcels, but such term shall apply only to Single Parcels, in separate Packages.

For the Carriage of any one Boiler, Cylinder, or Single Piece of Machinery, or Single Piece of Timber or Stone, or other Single Article, the Weight of which, including the Carriage, shall exceed Four Tons but shall not exceed Eight Tons, *Twelvepence* per Ton per Mile.

For the Carriage of any Single Piece of Timber, Stone, Machinery, or other Single Article, the Weight of which, with the Carriage, shall exceed Eight Tons, the Company will demand such sum as they think fit.

All which TOLLS the said Company direct and appoint to be paid in advance to the Company's Collectors at the Stations from which the Traffic departs, or, in the Company's option, on demand at the Stations to which it is destined.

BY ORDER OF THE DIRECTORS,

GLASGOW, 28th February, 1854.   J. FAIRFULL SMITH, *Secretary.*

HEDDERWICK & SON, PRINTERS TO THE QUEEN.

The G&SWR leased the Kilmarnock & Troon Railway in 1846 and set about re-gauging and modernising it. (Stenlake Collection) anomalous element in national life. Future difficulties lay in wait because of this ambiguous status, but in 1845 a huge railway bonanza was getting under way.

Railways to Everywhere

You could not open a newspaper in 1845 without finding news of railway plans along with advertisements to lure readers into investing in new lines, always described as having the most excellent prospects. On 29th September that year an entire page of the *Scotsman* was taken up by a list of Bills to be presented to Parliament for new railways. With the exception of the railways north and west of Inverness, and the line from Crianlarich to Fort William and Mallaig, by the end of that year virtually every line subsequently constructed in Scotland had been proposed, though many years would elapse before some of them were built. Others were never built at all. Learmonth was prominent, with another of his projects being a railway from Edinburgh to Hawick. He was also chairman of the Edinburgh & Northern Railway, starting from a ferry terminal at Burntisland, and running across Fife to Cupar. Determined to get control of the railways in Fife, he ran huge financial risks to achieve it, putting £90,000 of North British capital into another proposed line, the Edinburgh & Perth, from North Queensferry via Kinross, without telling the NBR shareholders. A whole set of trends was rising to a climax. Falling interest rates made it easier to borrow money, manufacturing industry was growing fast, and there was a sense of confidence in the future. Britain was embracing its role as the world's prime industrial nation, and railways were seen as a safe investment. Magazines were launched to advise people on new railway schemes and how to buy shares. Towns without a railway link wanted one urgently, preferably on a main line, though a branch was better than nothing. Without a railway, they feared loss of commerce, population decline, even extinction. Seeing newcomers propose lines that conflicted with their own future plans, existing railway companies vigorously promoted their own schemes. Meanwhile the value of railway shares kept on rising.

Gushetfaulds in 1848, with the embankment works of the Glasgow, Barrhead & Neilston Direct Railway. Painting by William Simpson (1823-99). (Hutton Collection)

It was possible to borrow a few hundred pounds, buy railway shares on which only a one-tenth deposit had to be paid, then sell the shares at a higher price to someone else and pocket a tidy profit – or do the same again. This became known as the 'Railway Mania' – and Parliament, which had to formally approve all new public railways, was flooded with proposals, many of them for competing routes between the same places.

The frenzy could not continue. The cost of proposed railways was greater than the country's entire capital. Sir Robert Peel informed the House of Commons that 107 railway Bills had been put forward for Scotland alone. Their total capital requirement was £28,500,000. Plenty of other ventures clamoured for investment: factories, ironworks, insurance corporations. Parliament sanctioned more than 423 miles of new railway in Scotland, and far more in England, during 1845. In January 1846 the bubble burst. Railway shares first slumped, then collapsed in value, jeopardising well-planned and useful schemes along with hastily run-up and even fraudulent proposals.

Picking Up the Pieces

The newly-formed companies found that everything had changed. Interest rates rose sharply, the cost of everything had gone up, investors often would not, or simply could not, pay the instalments on shares that they had signed up for – many had suffered heavy losses or bankruptcy due to the Mania. Scottish railways approved in 1845 needed capital totalling some £8 million. Seven years of extreme financial difficulties lay ahead, and in 1850 it was found necessary to pass an Act "to facilitate abandonment of railways". For the fifteen companies with lines already up and running, things were less bad because at least they were earning from their traffic. By the end of 1850, the combined authorised capital and loans of the Aberdeen, Caledonian, Edinburgh & Glasgow, Glasgow & South Western, Great North, North British and Morayshire companies amounted to £26,328,811. The amount they had actually collected was £17,400,307. The Great North of Scotland Railway, with only £69,000 raised out of a required £2 million, had not even started construction.

Some building went ahead, on a more limited and frugal scale than had been anticipated, including the Caledonian Railway and the lines northwards to Perth and Aberdeen. On 10 September 1847 the Caledonian ran its first public train, from a temporary terminus at Beattock, to Carlisle, and in February 1848 the line was complete between Carlisle and Glasgow, with a branch to Edinburgh diverging at Carstairs. Initially the Caledonian used Glasgow's first terminus at Townhead, opened in 1831 by the Glasgow & Garnkirk Railway, which it had taken over; then briefly South Side in the Gorbals, jointly with the Glasgow, Barrhead and Neilston Railway, until Buchanan Street Station was opened in November 1849. The backers of the Glasgow, Dumfries & Carlisle Railway did not give up, and re-formed their organisation. The Greenock and Ayrshire companies shared a terminus at Bridge Street and the line to Paisley (Gilmour Street), and the Edinburgh & Glasgow Railway had had Queen Street since 1840. Glasgow's south bank docks were served by the Polloc & Govan Railway to Windmillcroft Dock (between 1840 and 1867) and the General Terminus & Glasgow Harbour Railway from 1848. Both of these were merged into the Caledonian system. Access to Buchanan Street from the south was somewhat circuitous, and as early as 1846 the lack of a north-south connection, and of a general exchange station, were exercising interested parties, who included Glasgow Town Council, the Clyde Trustees, and the Admiralty as well as the railway companies and their customers. Just where and how the Clyde should be bridged was the key question, though proposed routes through the already close-packed and slum-ridden centre were also a source of controversy. Four Parliamentary Select Committees and one Royal Commission considered these questions in 1846. Each company's scheme was shot down by the others, while the Admiralty and Clyde Trustees made their own difficulties.

From early 1848 a Caledonian line branched from Garnqueen, north of Coatbridge, to meet the Edinburgh & Glasgow Railway at Greenhill. In May the Scottish Central Railway opened between Greenhill and Perth. Perth already had a railway to Dundee, and from 1 August the Scottish Midland Junction Railway would open through Strathmore to Forfar. Joining there with the Arbroath & Forfar Railway, it only needed the completion of the Aberdeen Railway, achieved on 1 April 1850, to have the whole West Coast Route established.

The World's First Train Ferries

The East Coast was very close behind. In 1849 the Royal Border Bridge was built across the Tweed Estuary at Berwick and with the opening in 1850 of the High Level Bridge over the Tyne at Newcastle, a complete railway existed between Edinburgh and London. In 1849 the North British branch to Hawick was finished, and some were already calling for its extension to Carlisle (though other voices said it would never pay its way). North of Edinburgh, the Firths of Forth and Tay did not deter railway promoters. Edinburgh's 'General' or 'Joint' Station, between the new Waverley and old North Bridges, opened on 17 May 1847 to serve both North British and Edinburgh & Glasgow company trains. An adjoining station, Canal Street, at right angles to it, was terminus of a line going north via a tunnel to Leith and Granton, the ferry port for Burntisland. From 1849 this became part of the Edinburgh, Perth & Dundee Railway, which had the distinction of introducing the world's first train ferries, across the Firths of Forth and Tay, in 1850 and 1851. These were the brain-child of an up-and-coming young engineer, Thomas Bouch, later to achieve fame and notoriety. The boats carried goods wagons, not passenger coaches, but nevertheless here was an integrated Edinburgh-Dundee service, with a link via Arbroath and Friockheim to the Aberdeen Railway. The network was widening, but the men who led the expansion would pay the price of their boldness.

Rocky Years

Financial strain almost broke the companies, with operating costs and new projects mopping up revenues. In 1849 North British £25 shares could be had for less than half-price, and this was typical. That year the NBR imposed pay cuts on its workers and almost all the drivers and firemen quit. Works mechanics and new recruits replaced them. The Caledonian, at that time the largest of the companies, having made a complex series of deals and leases with other railways, found itself on the brink of financial collapse. An attempt to get the London & North Western Railway to work the line failed, and in February 1850 Hope-Johnstone and his fellow-directors resigned. A special Act of Parliament was obtained in August in order to give the company a breathing space against its creditors.

Up until 1849 the Aberdeen and Great North of Scotland companies had separate boards but the same men as directors. The Aberdeen Railway, forced by lack of funds to suspend building work, joined with six other Scottish companies to ask the government for a loan of £1,000,000. The government refused: railway companies had to stand or fall on their own feet. After revelations of dodgy share dealing by some directors of the cash-strapped company, the Aberdeen's board was reformed and several members, including Sir James Elphinstone, chaiman of the still un-begun GNSR, departed from it. From then on, the two Aberdeen-based companies were enemies, agreeing on only thing: to abandon the original plan to amalgamate themselves into one. On the Ayrshire Railway, just over a year after declaring a handsome 7% dividend for the half-year to 31 January 1847, James McCall and his board were forced to resign after a highly adverse report from a shareholders' committee. Their manoeuvres in buying up other lines, sometimes with the aim of shutting them down, covering up losses, and meeting the demands of the extension from Cumnock to Dumfries and Gretna, were remorselessly exposed. The *Glasgow Herald* commented that it was surprising they had not gone long ago, "considering what a peck of troubles they have landed the shareholders in". On the North British, where also the company's debts had risen above its assets, John Learmonth survived as chairman until May 1852, resigning after fierce attacks by London-based shareholders.

It took a special kind of individual to be chairman of one of Scotland's early railway companies. He had to be personally wealthy and willing to risk his wealth, persuasive but also forceful, shrewd as well as bold, prepared to devote much of his time and energy to this new and intensely competitive business which required the instincts of a pirate, the strategic vision of a field marshal, and the demagogic skills of a popular orator. They had to be fighters, and like fighters they went down. Vilified by shareholders and the press, they left a reputation for bad management which was not altogether their fault. These were the men who got the network started. It was not their job to co-operate and create a sensible, shared railway system that would serve the country's present and future needs, but to defend, preserve and expand their own companies, and they did it in the only ways open to them. If they had not fought, they would have been eaten up. The Caledonian's ruthless drive to extend its system across the country, easily represented as empire-building or commercial greed, had a certain logic in its attempt to outflank the competition from the start.

Most of the first generation of railway directors lost money rather than getting rich (as they doubtless had hoped to do). Anyone who admires the superb viaduct of the G&SWR at Ballochmyle, masterpiece of the railway engineer John Miller, should spare a thought for James McCall. The builders of the new Borders Railway found that much of the work of John Learmonth's engineers, done while he battled to keep the construction money flowing in, was still usable for their new track in the 21st century.

John Miller (1805-83), engineer, architect and entrepreneur, was responsible for the planning of more than 20 Scottish railways, including the Edinburgh & Glasgow Railway, and for the design of many fine viaducts. (Courtesy Scottish Borders Council. ICE Scotland Museum, Heriot-Watt University)

Competition and Expansion – the 1850s

New Men in Charge

Railway companies had a rough time in the late 1840s and early 50s, but the lines kept on working, even if engines and rolling stock carried plates naming them as the property of banks and insurance companies which had lent enormous sums. And the benefits of the expanding network were being felt. Along the line of the 'Ayrshire' it was noted that thriving villages were replacing "clusters of huts", and Glasgow's ever-growing population, around 350,000 in 1847, was receiving fresh farm produce daily from places more than 30 miles away. Commercial prospects were improving. North Lanarkshire production of pig-iron rose from 39,000 tons in 1830 to 564,000 tons in 1848, and annual coal output at the end of the 1840s approached 10 million tons. In an indication of the spreading network, most Scottish companies joined the Railway Clearing House in 1850. This very useful organisation had been founded in London in 1842 to allow one charge to be made for goods or passengers whose journey involved more than one railway, with the revenue apportioned among the companies whose lines were traversed. It was hoped that the 1850s, with a new generation of directors in charge, would be a decade of steady growth and improvement. The new men, promising transparency, financial responsibility, and prudence, found very soon that it was not as easy as they thought.

Four of the five companies that would eventually take over all Scottish railways were already in existence in 1850, though one, the Great North of Scotland, was still

Crests of the five main pre-grouping railways. Clockwise from top left: Caledonian Railway crest 1840s; the crest of the Highland Railway Company (1865) combines the arms of Inverness and Perth; crest of the Great North of Scotland Railway, showing the arms of City of Aberdeen with the Scottish lion rampant; crest of the Glasgow & South Western Railway Company, established in 1850; and the crest of the North British Railway, originally of the Edinburgh & Berwick, showing the arms of Edinburgh and Berwick on Tweed.

no more than a name. The north's first railway was the Morayshire, between Lossiemouth and Elgin, in August 1852, followed by the Deeside Railway from Aberdeen to Banchory in September 1853. The Caledonian was still teetering on the edge of bankruptcy, with the Glasgow & South Western, formed in October 1850 by merger of the Ayrshire with the completed Glasgow, Dumfries & Carlisle Railway, in an equally parlous state. The North British had assets of £275,623 and obligations of £395,406 and its shareholders were at war with the directors. Only the Highland Railway did not yet exist. An Inverness group had applied in 1845 for a line to run through the Grampians to Perth, which had been rejected by a Parliamentary committee, unable to believe a railway could be made over such an "Alpine" route; and the post-Mania disenchantment with railway investment held further efforts in check until 1853.

Company Relations

At the end of 1852 there were no railways south of Ayr and west of Dumfries, though several were under consideration. Development of the lines in this region reveal the problems facing those who sought railway links. Where there were coal or iron mines, or big towns, or factories, it was relatively easier to raise money for railway building and for the railway to be profitable. The mines around Cumnock and Sanquhar helped to justify the Kilmarnock-Dumfries line, and the Dalmellington mines plus the prospect of an ironworks got a railway built along the Doon Valley in 1856. The Glasgow & South Western Railway backed a proposal for an Ayr-Maybole-Girvan railway and another for a line from Castle Douglas to Dumfries. Andrew Orr, second chairman of the South Western, expected these to be self-financing extensions of his system, but local support was far short of what was needed, and his company had to contribute heavily. A grander project was also proposed. Portpatrick was the east end of the shortest sea-crossing to Ireland, and a hitherto sparse traffic between there and Donaghadee was growing as Belfast became industrialised and demanded a better mail service. This could be provided by a railway from Portpatrick to join the Glasgow-London route at Dumfries, and a forceful Wigtownshire grandee, Viscount Dalrymple (later Earl of Stair), was the moving spirit in setting up the British & Irish Grand Junction Railway committee, encouraged by an Admiralty report confirming Portpatrick-Donaghadee as the best route for a mail service. Surely the Post Office would pay handsomely for carriage of the mails. Mail had been an important factor in railway finances from the start, especially when the line ran for many miles across thinly-populated country. Dalrymple's company, prosaically renamed the Portpatrick Railway, obtained its Act in August 1857.

At the opposite corner of the country, the Great North of Scotland Railway, founded to reach Inverness, finally opened to Huntly in September 1854 and to Keith in October 1856. Here it stalled, with too little money to continue. Inverness, which had opened a line to Nairn in November 1855, now filled the gap, completing the Inverness & Aberdeen Junction Railway via Elgin to Keith in August 1858. At first there was some participation by the Great North in this venture, but friction between the companies – the Great North nursed ambitions for lines beyond Inverness, which the Inverness party, with their own plans for a line into Ross-shire, had no intention of permitting – resulted in the Great North's interest being bought out in 1860. After that, hostile relations would prevail for nearly forty years. With the Great North refusing to collaborate with its neighbouring companies, Aberdeen was an inconvenient place to change trains or trans-ship goods.

After a couple of uncertain years, a new era for the North British Railway began with the election in 1855 of the energetic Richard Hodgson as chairman, the first Englishman to chair a Scottish railway, from just over the Tweed, at Carham. Ambitious and none too fastidious in his business methods, Hodgson immediately began planning the extension of the railway from Hawick to Carlisle, to secure NBR access to both the East Coast and West Coast routes. A four-year battle followed with the Caledonian, which also wanted the line to Hawick, and even more to keep the North British out of Carlisle. At huge expense to both companies, victory eventually went to the North British. Other lines proposed or sponsored by the NBR, and worked by it, spread across the Borders and Fife, and although it gained much traffic, Hodgson's expansionism ensured that costs ran high and profits were small. In anticipation of its arrival in Carlisle, the North British gained control of two local English railways, the Port Carlisle and Silloth lines, and became owner of Silloth Docks.

Having spent the first years of the 1850s extricating itself from a financial morass, the Caledonian by mid-1853 was looking around for new opportunities. Amalgamation with the Edinburgh & Glasgow Railway was proposed, then withdrawn. Instead the two companies waged a price war on their Glasgow-Edinburgh routes, taking the inter-terminus fare down to sixpence, though passengers joining at intermediate points paid the full amount, to their fury (an identical tactic would be employed by ScotRail, fighting coach competition, 150 years later). If the North British was making the running in expanding its network, by 1856 the Caledonian was also laying new railways, in the Lanarkshire coal district to Lesmahagow and Coalburn and around Motherwell. In 1859 its board elected a new chairman, another Border Englishman, Thomas Salkeld, a Cumberland landowner.

Parliament Flexes its Muscles

Finding in the later 1840s that it was hopeless trying to raise capital by issuing more Ordinary shares, due to minimal or non-existent dividends, railway

North British workers at Eastfield Locomotive Depot, Glasgow, with No. 153 *Glen Fruin*. Built in 1917, it was withdrawn in October 1959 as BR No. 62480. (Stenlake Collection)

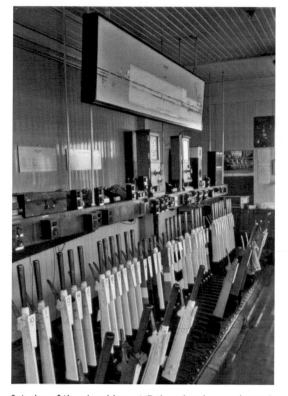

Interior of the signal box at Dalry, showing equipment in use prior to the electrification of the Ayr lines in the mid-1980s. (Stenlake Collection)

companies had to find new ways of raising money for new projects, adding to the grievances of the original shareholders by a steady elaboration of the railway share market. Preference shares, offering a fixed or 'guaranteed' return of 5% or more a year, were issued. These of course took precedence in the payment queue and the original, now "Ordinary", shares fell even further in value. Even if a company could not pay its Preference dividend, the unpaid amount accrued to the next period, with interest. Debenture issues, essentially loans repayable by a specified date and at an attractive rate of interest, went right to the head of the queue. Only once these had been paid were the Ordinary shareholders considered. In theory, their shares had no upper limit of dividend but in practice they rarely got more than 3% a year and often nothing at all. People who had bought £50 Ordinary shares for £100 or more now found they were hard to sell even at a loss.

The companies' need to focus on their own problems made the 1850s a relatively quiescent time, helped by Parliament's disinclination to authorise amalgamations, preferring to encourage fixed-term deals between companies, like line leases, or joint purses in which the proceeds of traffic on competing routes could be shared on an agreed basis. Edward Cardwell, President of the Board of Trade, pointed out that the whole tendency of railway companies was towards union and extension: not competition but monopoly. Sympathising with the concern of traders about what enlarged railway companies might do, his Railway & Canal Traffic Act of 1854 compelled the railways to provide proper facilities for receiving and forwarding traffic; to not discriminate unreasonably between customers; and to facilitate interchange without delays or obstructions. Among the few amalgamations of the period was that of the Aberdeen and Scottish Midland Junction companies in 1856, forming the Scottish North Eastern Railway, linking Perth, Forfar and Aberdeen.

At the end of 1859 Scotland had 49 railway companies, most of them financially and operationally dependent on a larger one, with 1,428 route miles. Their authorised capital and loans amounted to £41,965,597. In the year 16,493,291 passenger journeys were made, bringing in receipts of £1,001,396. Goods, mail and parcels traffic brought in almost double that sum, £1,923,333. Just over 6,300 people were employed. A useful extra source of income came from public use of lineside telegraph wires, set up originally for company communication and train control. Stations doubled as telegraph offices and often post offices as well.

Consolidation and Combination – the 1860s

A System that Needs Sorting

From the early 1860s, most people with an interest in the matter were agreed that some rationalisation of the railway companies was necessary. The economy, the population, the scale of commerce all were growing. Ever more people travelled, a widening range of commodities and consumer goods was being carried, and public expectations of the railway service had rapidly moved from gratitude at having a railway at all to critical intolerance of any perceived shortcomings of the system. Railways by now were the basic means of inland transport not only for bulk freight like coal, iron ore, fertilisers, timber, and livestock, but for everything else from hogsheads of whisky to grandfather clocks and pots and pans. They were "common carriers" (in Scots law "public carriers") who by offering a public transportation service at set prices could not turn away any passenger or consignment of goods as long as there was sufficient accommodation and due payment was made. A new public attitude was discernible: railways had made themselves so much a part of life that places not on the network felt that they ought to be provided with a railway connection as a sort of natural right, like a road. Rather than hazard their own cash, local feeling was that the construction cost should be met by the railway company, which after all would make money by running the trains.

Among the companies, genuine independents included the Scottish Central, the Scottish North Eastern, the Monklands Railways (a consortium of some of the oldest central lines, doing well on coal haulage), and the Portpatrick Railway. This last had opened in 1861, confounding the expectations of the G&SWR by deciding first to run its own trains – not successfully – and then in 1864 making a deal with the Caledonian, which agreed to work its line for 21 years, on terms which left it with a net loss. But the Caledonian's blue engines could now be seen from Aberdeen to remotest Galloway. Things had not worked out altogether as planned for the 'Port

A Caledonian 0-4-2 engine of 1860s vintage on the Tay Viaduct at Perth, showing the bridge as rebuilt in 1863. The swing span was rarely used after the 1870s. (Stenlake Collection)

Road': in 1865 the Government abandoned its efforts to improve Portpatrick Harbour and Stranraer became the port for passengers as well as goods and cattle, leaving Portpatrick at the end of a branch line. By 1860 a line ran south from Ayr through Maybole as far as Girvan, and completion of the Glasgow-Stranraer-Dumfries triangle looked imminent. A Girvan & Portpatrick Junction Railway company was formed, but found few investors, and another seventeen years would elapse before it finally opened.

The Mergers

The Edinburgh & Glasgow Railway was still one of the bigger players, now including lines from Stirling to Dunfermline (1858) and from Glasgow to Dumbarton and Helensburgh, north of the city centre by way of Cowlairs and Maryhill (1862). Parliament refused a merger between it, the Caledonian, and Scottish Central Railways in 1861 and again in 1864. The Caledonian had a hopeful eye on the Edinburgh & Glasgow's Dunfermline line, which offered an entry into the North British enclave of Fife, and the North British spent heavily to oppose these merger proposals. Parliament's hostility to monopoly was weakening under pressure from the many members with railway directorships or investments: at this time, the 'railway interest' was as strong and demanding as the 'road lobby' would be in the 1930s. Although among politicians and the general public there was still a deep-seated unease about monopoly businesses, larger groupings were no longer out of the question, and in 1863-66 the Scottish railway scene changed dramatically.

The prospect of mightily expensive battles for who-gets-what encouraged diplomatic talks, but a general agreement was impossible. Instead, through inter-company deals, a rapid succession of mergers ensued. Taking place at a time of renewed financial difficulty (bank rate hit 10% for three months in 1866) the amalgamations did not happen peaceably, arousing great controversy among shareholders, goods shippers, and the wider public. The North British absorbed the Edinburgh, Perth & Dundee in 1862; the Scottish Central took over the Dundee & Perth & Aberdeen Railway (really only Dundee to Perth) in 1863, and was itself amalgamated with the Caledonian in July 1865. In 1866 the Caledonian also took over the Scottish North Eastern, gaining ownership of the entire Glasgow-Perth-Forfar-Aberdeen route and its multiple branches. On 31 July 1865 the Edinburgh & Glasgow company took over the Monklands Railways and on the following day it was amalgamated into the North British. The NBR and Caledonian emerged from the process as relative giants, and with a tangle of intersecting lines in the Stirlingshire-North Lanarkshire mining area.

Developments North and South

The railways of the north and south west were not involved in the amalgamations. In the north east, the Great North was in a crisis of its own making. Shut off at Keith, it had busied itself in setting up branches in Buchan and Banffshire, and in 1856 it had opened an Aberdeen terminus at Waterloo Quay, ignoring an original commitment to sharing a joint central station with the Aberdeen Railway at Guild Street. In 1862 it took control of the Deeside Railway, which had been extended to Aboyne in 1859 and would reach its final terminus at Ballater in 1866. By then branches had spread to Fraserburgh, Peterhead, Banff, Macduff, Old Meldrum and Alford, as well as an alternative line from Keith to Elgin via Dufftown. In 1863 the Great North opened the scenic, very costly and woefully unprofitable Strathspey Railway from Craigellachie to Boat of Garten, in an effort to tap traffic from the new Inverness-Perth railway. Investment in this proliferation of mostly low-return branch lines almost bankrupted the company by 1865.

Its failure to provide a north-south connection in Aberdeen helped to make the case for a direct Inverness-Perth line, which was finally approved in 1861, swiftly built, and opened in 1863. Now there was a main line reaching directly from central Scotland to the far north. It snapped up the postal contract from the Great North, along with the growing summer traffic; and in 1865 the Inverness & Perth and Inverness & Aberdeen Railways combined to form the Highland Railway Company, putting the fifth of the Big Five in place. Already its northern arm was at Bonar Bridge, and the enthusiastic backing and huge financial resources of the Duke of Sutherland (based on Staffordshire coal mines) would push successive extensions through to the northern termini of Thurso and Wick. For pessimists, the Highland Railway simply provided an easy means of emigration from a ravaged region; for optimists like the Duke, it offered a lifeline for regeneration – a theme that would replay 100 years later. Belatedly, the Great North built a line through Aberdeen from Kittybrewster to Guild Street (by then a Caledonian terminus) in 1867, and a new joint station was finally built.

The Glasgow & South Western was kept busy protecting its territory from further Caledonian intrusion. It provided a classic example of new-line building not based on actual requirements but in order to keep another company at bay, with a Parliamentary Bill in November 1864 listing eleven proposed lines designed to frustrate the Caledonian's aim to extend its Carstairs-Douglas branch to Muirkirk and Ayr, so providing an Ayr-Edinburgh railway. Andrew Orr, by 1864, was almost as much embroiled in expensive new schemes as his predecessor had been fifteen years before. In March 1865 an agreement was made between the two companies to avoid "antagonistic" schemes in Ayrshire. In the following March the South Western board came up with a surprise: a proposal to merge with the English Midland Railway. The Glasgow & South Western had always had slim pickings at Carlisle, where the Caledonian and London & North Western jointly owned the passenger station, but now the Midland was going to build another Anglo-Scottish main line, from Leeds (the present Settle & Carlisle) and there was promise of a leap in both goods and passenger traffic. But the Bill was rejected, probably because the Midland's line did not yet exist (it was not completed until 1875).

The Big Five

The basic territories of the Big Five were now staked out: the Highland north of Perth and west of the Grampians; the Great North in Aberdeenshire, Banffshire and Moray; the Glasgow & South Western south and west of the Clyde and Annan rivers; the Caledonian in a broad arc from Carlisle to Aberdeen; and the North British in the centre, Fife and the south east. There would be penetrations and cross-lines, but the essential dispensation remained until 1923. Not the least remarkable aspect of the mergers was that the companies were all in serious financial difficulties again, having spent, and borrowed, hugely in promoting and building their own projects and opposing those of others. Turmoil in the North British Railway's affairs saw Richard Hodgson voted out of office as chairman in 1866 after exposure of manipulation of the accounts and illegal payment of dividends from capital. Along with the public battle against the Caledonian, he had been keeping up a campaign to conceal the dire reality of the company's affairs from the shareholders and even from his co-directors.

A year later, the Caledonian chairman Thomas Salkeld resigned in stormy circumstances, with a slumped share price and a rump board after six directors quit. His resignation, and Hodgson's even more so, marked the end of the era of the all-

Train crossing the pier-like lattice of the Solway Viaduct. (Stenlake Collection)

dominant chairman. A Royal Commission on Railways sat in 1865-67 and though it largely maintained the state's *laisser-faire* approach, it set new and stricter standards for accounting and reporting, limiting opportunities for manipulation of the figures to justify policies which shareholders would have seen as against their interests. Competition and rivalry did not cease by any means, but the companies were now larger and more mature, and senior officials, particularly the general managers, more influential. Managers and superintendents were by now used to meeting in organisations like the Clearing House, and at the regular conferences of the companies which formed the East Coast and West Coast routes, where a series of agreements was made on the division of Anglo-Scottish freight and passenger traffic.

Before his ousting from the NBR, Richard Hodgson had seen the triumphant opening of the Hawick-Carlisle line in June 1862, immediately named the Waverley Route; and had obtained an Act in 1865 for another grand ambition, the construction of a great bridge across the Firth of Forth. Edinburgh's General Station, known as Waverley from the late 1850s, had become inadequate for its traffic, and a programme of rebuilding, with a new Waverley Bridge, began in 1866. Expansion of Waverley would be a regular topic of controversy between railway and town council into the 21st century. Among other new routes at this time, a third Edinburgh-Glasgow railway was opened by the Caledonian in 1869, via Mid Calder, and a new Anglo-Scottish link was formed by the Solway Junction Railway, intended to carry Cumbrian iron ore to Scottish ironworks (Scottish ore deposits were virtually worked out by this time). Its iron bridge across the Solway Firth, then the longest in Britain at 1,940 yards, never achieved iconic status.

The Telegraph Act of 1868, which placed telegraphs under national ownership, provided the companies with a useful cash bonus in exchange for handing over their telegraph lines, with railway use continuing on their own wires. By the end of the decade, the basis of the railway network was complete. Apart from Wick and Thurso, and Dunoon and Campbeltown at the ends of their peninsulas, no mainland towns of any size were now without railway connection. A very large area remained unpenetrated in the western and north western Highlands, where despite population clearance that had been going on for over thirty years, some districts still had a quite substantial though dispersed population. Any railway provision there would mean investment in long extension lines. The era of the deer forest was just beginning and it was not a territory that promised much margin of profit over working costs. Already, though, there was agitation for better communication, not least for a faster mail service to link up with island steamers. In the later 1860s, two 'extension' lines were authorised, one between Callander, terminus of a Caledonian branch, and Oban (population in 1861 just under 2000); the other from the Highland line at Dingwall to Kyle of Lochalsh (population a few dozen). Some other gaps existed, notably on the Banffshire coast between Elgin and Banff, where a string of fishing villages might be linked in to help supply a growing demand – itself a result of railway speed – for fresh fish.

Glasgow in the 1860s

The first railway bridge over the Clyde in the Glasgow area was well upstream at Dalmarnock, carrying a Caledonian goods branch from Rutherglen in 1861 to serve factories on the east of the city, too far out to help resolve the problems in the centre. By the early 1860s there was still no lower bridge. Civic improvement was becoming a major theme and the city's termini offered the opposite of a good impression. Town councillors complained volubly. Buchanan Street was not the worst. The South Side terminus was described as "a discredit to the city". Bridge Street's cramped space with four platform faces had to cope with over two million people a year by the later 1850s. Even in 1870 Queen Street only had two platforms for passenger trains.

As before, each time a railway company proposed a solution, usually including a Clyde crossing and "grand central" passenger and goods station, it was vetoed by the others. The Glasgow & South Western and the Caledonian, though they had an agreement to share the English traffic at Carlisle, were on bad terms. The Edinburgh & Glasgow company was fighting Caledonian attempts to expand in Lanarkshire.

All this made a concerted policy in Glasgow very difficult. A new plan was put forward in late 1863, authored by the engineers John Fowler (later of Forth Bridge fame) and J.F. Blair. Their City of Glasgow Union Railway would run from Shields Junction across the southern part of the city, then swing north, crossing the river to link up with incoming lines and also provide a north bank "Union Railway Terminal" at St. Enoch Square, to provide a joint station for the Caledonian, Edinburgh & Glasgow, and Glasgow & South Western, with links to all their lines. Project management was assumed by the South Western and Edinburgh & Glasgow, offering somewhat restricted access to the Caledonian

Scotland's 'oldest' station. A medieval building Glasgow's the High Street was used as the College Station office from 1866 to 1870. (Author's Collection)

on a take-it-or-leave it basis. The Caledonian declined, and actively opposed the scheme, which was however passed by Parliament in 1864. The Caledonian then decided to build its own north bank terminus, though it did not rush into action. Congestion of trains, carts, omnibuses and passengers remained the norm for several more years, and Glasgow's hope for a large central interchange station would remain permanently unfulfilled.

Did the inadequacy of terminal facilities in the 1850s and 60s do anything to cramp Glasgow's industrial and commercial development? The likelihood is that it hardly did at all. There was inconvenience, and annoyance, but one of the reasons the stations were so crowded was that many more trains were being run. Goods services were improved; in 1864 the Caledonian built a five-storey grain warehouse and a nine-bay goods shed at Buchanan Street, further eclipsing the passenger terminal. Complaints from traders were less about delays (except in the case of perishable items, which the railways usually managed to expedite) than about breakages of fragile items and the companies' rates for haulage and delivery. The ups and downs of the wider economy were more significant than railway facilities. Glaswegians might fret and complain, but with each year they gained daily contact with more and more places throughout Britain.

In 1870, route mileage had reached 2397. A total of 1,241 engines ran 9,463,114 miles with passenger trains and 12,352,060 miles with freight, using 2,564 carriages, 801 other passenger train vehicles (luggage and fish trucks), 43,701 goods vehicles and 475 assorted others. Several thousand goods wagons were also owned by private companies, usually collieries or coal merchants. Passenger journeys numbered 27,044,854, with a revenue of £1,780,652. Goods brought in £2,872,285. Working expenses were almost exactly 50% of revenue. The total capital invested was now £65,512,297 with a further £16,873,552 in debentures and loans. Not all of that amount had been spent on installations and equipment – much had been poured into the coffers of law firms and Parliamentary counsel, or into investments in failed projects, and by now represented no actual value at all.

Motive Power and Rolling Stock Up To 1870

Horse traction lingered on one isolated railway, the Paisley & Renfrew, until 1866, when the Glasgow & South Western, whose predecessors had owned it since 1847, regauged it from 4ft 4in to the national standard of 4ft 8½in, and linked it to the national network. By the mid-1840s, there was really no task on Scottish railways that locomotives of the time could not perform. Even on the steep, tunnelled incline from Glasgow Queen Street, engines could have done it (and briefly did, in the 1840s) but the railway company liked the security of the supplementary hauling cable that survived until 1908. Locomotives were built by foundries in Greenock, Glasgow and Dundee, but the railway companies set up their own works from early days. Every railway that aspired to run its own trains had to have workshops where engines could be serviced and repaired, and even built. The Edinburgh & Glasgow Railway established Cowlairs Works in Glasgow in 1841, which the North British took over in 1865, in addition to its St. Margaret's Works (1846) in Edinburgh. The Caledonian moved from Greenock to set up St. Rollox Works (Glasgow) in 1853 and also had workshops at Perth. Workshops for the Great North of Scotland were set up at Kittybrewster in 1852. The Glasgow & South Western shops moved from Cook Street in Glasgow to a larger site at Kilmarnock in 1856. Smaller workshops at Dundee and Arbroath did not survive the amalgamations of the 1850s and 1860s, but the North British kept on the old Edinburgh Perth & Dundee works at Burntisland for repair work, partly because of the Forth water gap that existed until the Forth Bridge opened in 1890, and also because of its intensive traffic in the Fife coalfield.

The companies designed and built much of their own rolling stock, especially passenger carriages. Much of the wagon stock came from outside builders, primarily in Scotland, who also hired out wagons at busy times. Carriages were four-wheelers, divided into four compartments. They were not heated, and lighting was provided by oil 'pot-lamps' set in the carriage roofs. Coach-building was a craft, and while third class carriages were as basic as possible, second class was well-padded and first class could be quite sumptuous, with the most splendid being the carriages of the East Coast Joint Stock, introduced in 1860 and jointly owned by the North British and the English East Coast companies. A brake van was required on each passenger train and it was the guard's responsibility to apply its brakes on gradients or on a warning whistle from the driver.

Locomotives for Scottish railways in the 1840s and 1850s were no different to those built for England, and many came from English builders. Most railways painted their engines in a shade of green, though the Caledonian opted for blue. At first most were lightweight machines, four-wheeled or with a single set of driving wheels, and weighing around 10 tons. By the later 1850s the most powerful new engines weighed around 30 tons. A distinction was made between passenger engines, usually of the 2-2-2 kind, and goods engines, usually four-coupled. Brakes were rudimentary, hand-operated and fitted only to the locomotive tender. Designers had to obey the stipulations of the civil engineer on the maximum weight per axle, as the original iron rails could be quite light. The Dundee & Arbroath had rails weighing 48lbs per yard, while the Edinburgh & Glasgow, an express route from the start, had rails of 74lbs per yard. All engines were legally obliged to "consume their own smoke" which meant burning coke rather than coal, though by 1860 the regulation was generally ignored. Trains were lightweight and express speeds rarely went above 50 mph.

Given the financial problems endemic to the railways, rebuilding of older engines became an important part of the mechanical engineers' work from the mid-1850s. Often, however, "rebuild" was used to describe what was virtually a new engine, since that could be charged to operating expenses rather than the capital account which shareholders were anxious to keep down.

The Caledonian Railway's No. 87 passenger locomotive with a 2-2-2 wheel configuration (two leading wheels, two driving wheels and two trailing wheels), built in 1865. (Stenlake Collection)

Maturity Sets In – the 1870s

New Lines and New Services

Standard procedure for building a new line was to set up a company, usually under the aegis of one of the Big Five, with its own local directors and capital account. When completed, the protecting company – by far the largest investor – would run the service and sooner or later absorb the new company, converting the shares into its own Preference stock. In 1870 the Dingwall & Skye Railway, backed by the Highland, succeeded at a last financial gasp in establishing the first west coast railhead north of Helensburgh, at Strome Ferry on Loch Carron. Despite hopes for industrial development on Lewis, its traffic would be small, revenue ranging from around £700 a week in July to under £100 in December. In July 1874 lines to the ultimate northern termini at Wick and Thurso were completed by local companies financed wholly or mainly by the Duke of Sutherland. Ten years later they would be absorbed into the Highland Railway, which ran the trains from the start. Independent companies working their own traffic were now very few. In 1870 the Forth & Clyde Junction (Stirling-Balloch) and Leven & East Fife were the only public railways operating their own engines and trains, and by 1877 both had been swallowed up by the North British. New lines included the briefly independent Glasgow, Bothwell, Hamilton & Coatbridge Railway, opened in 1874 from the NBR at Shettleston. Built with industrialists' money (primarily from the huge Baird coal and iron company) it was an aggressive project, intended to divert custom from Caledonian lines in the same area. In 1878 it was merged into the North British. In the far south west the Wigtownshire Railway was being built from Newton Stewart to Whithorn, completed in July 1877 and operating its own trains until 1885. Joint lines were uncommon, though under extreme pressure from shareholders the Caledonian and Glasgow & South Western abandoned plans for separate lines and combined in 1873 to extend the Barrhead line to Kilmarnock, making the direct Glasgow-Kilmarnock railway which had been locally wanted ever since the Ayrshire main line had gone round by Dalry.

Relations between the two largest companies veered between collaboration and confrontation. They could co-operate: until 1870 Caledonian trains from Glasgow to Perth via Stirling used Queen Street, and North British trains to Airdrie ran from Buchanan Street until 1871; and in 1871-2 the details of a merger were worked out, but mutual mistrust and intense opposition from commercial customers and town councils led to its being dropped. The North British chairman since 1866, John Stirling of Kippendavie, a keen supporter of amalgamation, believed that "either

John Stirling of Kippendavie, chairman of the North British Railway from 1866 to 1882. (Courtesy of Mr and Mrs Stirling-Aird)

Perhaps on their way to camp, a Boys Brigade troop, with piper and drummers, wait for the train at the North British Falkland Road Station. The year is around 1910. (Stenlake Collection)

the Scotch railways will be amalgamated into a large concern, or we shall be cut up and divided among the English lines". His fellow-chairmen may have shared this broad view, but customers and many shareholders did not.

Pressures for Improvement: New Termini for Glasgow at Last

Though some travellers preferred the sea breezes (and cheaper fares) of the coastal steamers between Leith and London, the railways held an almost-total monopoly of inland transport. Even the Forth & Clyde and Union Canals were now owned by the Caledonian and NBR respectively. Improvements to stations, resisted by boards because they were seen as not generating new revenue, were driven by competition on certain routes, especially for first class traffic, or by the need to enlarge them because of the ever-increasing numbers of third class passengers. Public toilets were provided because people would otherwise find a way of satisfying their needs on railway premises. Smoking was originally banned in all carriages, until the 1868 Railways Regulation Act laid down that all trains with more than one carriage must provide a smoking compartment for each class. Carriages were still unheated. Passengers on the Highland could hire rugs at Inverness, and foot warmers began to make an appearance on trains in the 1870s, at first only on competitive services. They resembled flat metal cushions, filled in platform boiler houses with heat-retaining acetate of soda.

In 1870 the Caledonian replaced its original Lothian Road terminus in Edinburgh with a new wooden building and renamed it Princes Street. At the other end, the North British was still rebuilding Waverley Station, the work completed in 1874 with a long central island platform and terminal bays at each end, and an access road running down from the rebuilt Waverley Bridge. Dundee, like Aberdeen until 1867, had no central station. In 1871, with construction starting on the Tay Bridge, the North British and Caledonian discussed a joint station, but abandoned the idea, and the NBR eventually built its own station.

Almost nothing had been done to improve Glasgow's main line termini. Between 1863 and 1873, usage of Queen Street Station went from one and a half million to three million passengers a year, with no increase in facilities. The companies might be in expansive mood but they preferred to build lines to create or capture extra traffic rather than engage in rebuilding of the termini, which would cost a lot without providing additional revenue. Both the Caledonian and North British put forward grand schemes, but kept them on paper. Public opinion might be hostile, and civic pride affronted, but the railways, secure in their monopoly of inland transport, were not too troubled. In the end they took action because the stations and access lines could not cope. More accommodation for trains and people simply had to be provided.

By the time the City of Glasgow Union Railway opened in 1870, the Edinburgh & Glasgow was merged with the North British, and the Union line joined the NBR at Bellgrove Station. A short spur led to a temporary Glasgow & South Western terminus at Dunlop Street, by St. Enoch Square. The South Western's long wait for the Midland Railway to reach Carlisle ended in 1875 and the great iron-framed arched train-shed of St. Enoch Station came into use from May 1876, serving the new route via Leeds and Carlisle. The old terminus at South Side, shared by the Caledonian and South Western, was partially demolished on the latter's side in 1877 and the rails carried onward to St. Enoch, by way of the City of Glasgow Union Railway. The Caledonian began preparations in 1873 to extend from its Bridge Street terminal platforms to a new site across the Clyde at Gordon Street, at the same time laying new tracks south of Bridge Street to meet the lines to Carlisle and to Barrhead and Kilmarnock. Glasgow Central opened for business on 1 August 1879. At a cost of £700,000, with eight platforms, it had been expected to satisfy traffic demands for years to come, but the city was growing so fast that it was immediately working to capacity. Rebuilding and enlarging of Queen Street Station, a ten-year process, finally began in 1878.

Government Concerns: Monopoly and Safety – the Tay Bridge Disaster

Renewed concerns about railway monopoly prompted the Government into appointing a Select Committee in 1872, which finally accepted that the whole tendency of railway history had been reduction, not promotion, of competition: "it has nevertheless become more and more evident that competition must fail to do for the railways what it has done for ordinary trade and that no means has yet been

Interior view of St. Enoch Station, Glasgow, in May 1966, with Platform I, departures indicator, and bookstall. (Stenlake Collection)

The original Tay Bridge (1871-79) seen from the south. The line to Tayport diverges to the right. (Stenlake Collection)

devised by which competition can be permanently maintained." In railway operation at least, the notion of a self-managing 'market' was laid to rest, until its semi-resurrection in 1994. The basis of railway rates and charges was still the Cardwell Act of 1854; and a new Act in 1873 created a Railway & Canal Commission, with judicial powers to regulate fares and charges. Despite all the tenets of freedom to trade, it was now accepted that railways were different. Henceforth, the companies' charges would be within the framework of official regulation.

Other concerns too were raised at this time. Faster and heavier trains presented safety problems which increasingly alarmed the travelling public, and the government began a twenty-year campaign to have continuous braking systems fitted to passenger trains, ensuring an automatic stop if carriages broke away. Despite pressure from the Board of Trade, the companies did little more than tinker with the issue through the 1870s. Here was another potential expense that would not generate additional revenue. The Caledonian tried the American-designed Westinghouse brake on the Wemyss Bay line, but also toyed with a system devised by its own brake inspector. In December 1876, Dugald Drummond, locomotive Superintendent of the North British, organised further tests in which Westinghouse proved superior, and the NBR was the first Scottish company to methodically set about fitting brakes, at least on express carriages.

Safety became a headline issue in 1879. For six years the North British had been building its viaduct across the Firth of Tay, and in June 1878 construction was completed. At 3,569 yards, it became the longest bridge in the world, and earned its designer Thomas Bouch a knighthood when Queen Victoria's train crossed it in June 1879. At the very end of that year the nation was horrified to learn that the central spans had collapsed in a gale, taking a passenger train down with them. Like no other accident, the disaster struck right to the core of Victorian complacency about Britain's engineering skill, managerial competence and commercial ethics. The North British board reacted with speed and efficiency to rearrange services, restore the train ferries, and prepare for the onslaught of claims from relatives of the 71 victims, and for the official inquiry. It announced almost immediately that the bridge would be rebuilt. Bouch was also designer of a Forth Bridge, on which preliminary work had been stopped in late 1879 for lack of funds. Following a damning official report on the causes of the Tay Bridge disaster, Bouch's reputation was shattered, his design was dropped, and the building contracts cancelled.

Taken for Granted – Employees and Shareholders

A railwaymen's trade union, the Amalgamated Society of Railway Servants, was established in England in 1871 and by 1872 it had a few branches in Scotland. Accustomed to dealing directly with their employees, the companies scorned the notion of a representative body, and ignored it. Questions of pay, discipline and grievance were handled directly by departmental heads, with reference to the boards only if a pay rise was recommended. In the entire period up to 1923, no company of its own free will granted a pay rise to its workers. The attitude was paternalistic, with chairmen liking to refer to the company as a family at annual staff functions; and in the spirit of the times, most staff willingly gave their commitment and loyalty. A railway job was regarded as more secure than most, with a uniform, and sometimes subsidised housing. Pensions, paid holiday time, sick pay, and compensation for injury did not exist. Working hours could be fourteen or more a day, without overtime pay. The rate of death and injury among workers was very high, and supervisors routinely blamed accidents on the victims' carelessness. Railwaymen, mostly dispersed at small centres, did not rush to join the union, which was strongest in Glasgow and Edinburgh.

With a new trade recession setting in, 1878 was a bad year for industrial relations. As traffic receipts fell, the companies began to enforce either pay cuts or extended hours. NBR workers at Cowlairs went on strike in April, followed by the Caledonian men at St. Rollox in June. Compromise was reached on the Caley, with a 51-hour working week and pay cuts of from 5% to 7.5%, but the dispute on the NBR, where a 54-hour week was enforced, ran on until the autumn, with the company hiring replacement workers, while at the same time ordering new carriages, wagons and engines to serve its new lines.

Shareholders had little in common with workmen, except that their presence in the scheme of things was also largely taken for granted. In theory of course, they were the owners of the company and much lip-service was paid to this at general meetings. Chairmen liked to refer to the "widows and orphans" who depended on Ordinary dividends, though throughout the 1870s a quarter of the companies' Ordinary shares received no dividend at all, and the real beneficiaries were the large institutions who held debentures. Shareholders would also be invited to attend special meetings in order to approve significant decisions, or drafts of Parliamentary Bills. Few normally turned up, even in the larger companies, though the Highland offered free tickets on its own system. Most simply entrusted their vote to participate to the chairman, who could thus usually command a majority in any case where there was disagreement. Real shareholder revolts were rare by now, though not unknown, and anxiety was always latent. A Scottish Railway Shareholders' Association was formed in 1873, at a time when the companies' proposed schemes would cost £8 million. Many people held shares in more than one company and were dismayed to see money being thrown away on competitive lines and services. Shareholder pressure helped to get a ten-year agreement in 1873 between the NBR and Caledonian on Edinburgh-Glasgow traffic, 80% to the North British and 20% to the Caledonian, which then dropped a plan to build its own line between Larbert and Edinburgh, which would have duplicated the North British line.

Public Service or Private Profit? – the 1880s

A Confident Start

The 1870s ended in another of the British economy's mysterious and apparently unavoidable cyclical slumps. By the end of 1880, things were recovering, with railway activity and investment reaching new heights. Mileage of Scottish lines had doubled in twenty years to 2,907 at the end of 1880, with 1,618 locomotives at work, 3,532 carriages and 1,243 other passenger vehicles, 83,013 goods vehicles, and 1171 assorted others. The number of passenger journeys made was 45,956,833, with receipts of £2,206,064. Tonnage of coal and minerals was 23,704,436, and of merchandise, 7,611,503, with combined receipts of £4,082,944. Working expenses were 51% of receipts, with 12,277,534 passenger train miles and 14,208,081 freight and mixed miles run. Total investment stood at £92,331,212.

Confidence abounded, and all companies were enlarging and improving their facilities for both goods and passengers. A programme of providing foot-bridges at double-line stations was put in hand from the late 1870s: iron bridges cost £205 apiece, wooden bridges, favoured for minor stations, were £85. Electric lighting was beginning to be installed in major stations and goods depots from 1881, and the telephone was coming into use at the same time. These were in part efficiency measures: electricity saved labour on gas or oil lighting, passengers injured crossing the lines sued for compensation and were rewarded by juries, and telephones hugely speeded up communication. However, cost-benefit analysis was still a long way off, and inter-company competition also figured in these developments. Both in the interest of passenger comfort and increased accommodation, bogie coaches came into use from 1886, first on the Caledonian's Glasgow-Edinburgh trains, with steam heating, gas lighting, and automatic brakes. New materials were also in use by the civil engineers. The short branch to Killin, off the Oban line, opened in March 1886, was the first in Scotland and one of the first in the world to have bridges with

Killin Station around 1920. The stationmaster was also in charge of Loch Tay Station. (Stenlake Collection)

The staff at Selkirk Station in the early 1900s. The stationmaster stands on the left. (Stenlake Collection)

concrete arches. Harbours were enlarged: in 1881 the North British completed a large new dock at Bo'ness for coal exports, and in the following year the Caledonian opened the new Carron Dock at Grangemouth to handle coal exports and timber and grain imports.

Through the 1880s the trend towards managerial control of the companies continued. Boards were increasingly supervisory, holding the balance between the various demands made on the company, while the general managers became the proposers of policy and held much more power. James Thompson, general manager of the Caledonian from 1882, would ultimately get a knighthood and become company chairman. John Walker, general manager of the NBR from 1874 until 1891, was very much the public face of the company. Andrew Dougall managed the Highland from 1865 to 1895, with an increasingly light hand from the board. Now very large, especially in the Scottish context, and rather complacent in their domination of inland transport, the companies needed efficient managers, steady helmsmen rather than visionary pilots.

Their evident prosperity was not lost on their employees, for whom busy times meant more work and long overtime, for which they were not paid. Locomotive crews and signalmen were routinely working 14 or 15-hour days, six days a week, and they reasonably pointed out the dangers to safety as well as the physical imposition. Better pay and conditions had been hard to argue for in the days when the companies were struggling, but now, though things were different, the boards did not yield easily. Caledonian men staged a short strike in January 1883 and North British workers achieved some concessions from a reluctant board. Eventually a succession of accidents made the Board of Trade take an interest in working hours. But the anger of the railway workers was sharpened by the 5% dividend paid to Caledonian Ordinary shareholders in March 1881, and the inauguration of a superannuation fund for senior management, part-funded by company money. Everyone was doing well out of the good times except them, it seemed.

English Involvements

In 1880 the Forth Bridge Railway Company entered a Bill for abandonment of its project, then withdrew it in 1881. The change of policy was due to Matthew Thompson, chairman of the Midland Railway, who organised a restructuring of the Bridge company, with the Midland taking a 32.5% share, NBR 30%, and the North Eastern and Great Northern Railways each taking 18.75% of the capital, reckoned then at £2 million. It was thus a 70% English enterprise. The new and massively imposing design by Benjamin Baker and John Fowler was accepted, and the contractor was William Arrol of Glasgow, who was also building the new Tay Bridge, a wholly North British project.

After long delays, in June 1880 the Callander & Oban Railway finally reached its western terminus on the Oban quayside, helped on its final stage by an investment of £50,000 from the London & North Western Railway. Excitement was aroused by a proposal originating in London in 1882 for a Glasgow & North Western Railway, to run via Loch Lomond, Glen Coe and the Great Glen to Inverness. Strong opposition from the Highland and Caledonian companies ensured that Parliament rejected the scheme, causing dismay in Fort William, where a railway link was felt to be long overdue. Such large investments and speculative interest from south of the Border reveal an expansive mood among the large English companies, and a belief in the economic prospects of lines through the Highlands which experience failed to justify. English money was also useful in the south west in 1885, when the Caledonian's agreement to run the trains to Stranraer and Portpatrick expired. Lord Stair negotiated the sale of the Portpatrick Railway to a consortium of the Caledonian, the G&SWR, the Midland, and the London & North Western Railways, to be run as a joint line, with himself as its chairman. The Wigtownshire Railway, independently worked until 1885, was included and the line became the Portpatrick & Wigtownshire Joint Railway. The two English companies were primarily

The Forth Bridge with its designers and building contractor. (Stenlake Collection)

The concourse at Perth General Station, in 1921 or 1922. (Stenlake Collection)

interested in the mail contract, and the Scottish companies took turns at running the trains and maintaining the tracks. Stair was probably the most successful of all Scottish railway chairmen, but he had only a single line to look after.

From 1886 the Girvan & Portpatrick, worked by the Glasgow & South Western since it opened in 1877, ran its own trains. Always struggling, legally insolvent, it was bought up and renamed the Ayrshire & Wigtownshire Railway by Anglo-Scottish speculators who exploited the rivalry between the South Western and the Caledonian by offering to sell it to the latter. The South Western eventually purchased the line in 1891 for much more than it wanted to pay, and also had to spend heavily to bring it up to a proper standard.

Expansion, Progress and Racing to the North

Perth General Station was completely rebuilt in 1884-85 by its three owners, the Caledonian, Highland and North British, in the form it still retains, though then nine platforms were in use. Dundee was growing fast as 'Juteopolis', but for the Caledonian, despite its size, it was on a branch, while the Tay Bridge had put the city on the North British Edinburgh-Aberdeen main line. The Caledonian built a new terminus, Dundee West, in the mid-1880s, close to the NBR's Tay Bridge Station. The new bridge, similar in outline to its predecessor, but double-track, and far more massive in construction, was opened on 11 July 1887. The railway from Dundee (East) to Arbroath was a joint Caledonian-NBR line from February 1880, as part of a deal relating to the Tay Bridge, and in the following year the North British completed a new line from Arbroath to a point beyond Montrose, joining the Caledonian line to Aberdeen at Kinnaber Junction, later to be a strategic location in the 'Races to the North'. Despite this new ground of competition, inter-company warfare was much reduced by now. The two biggest companies operated a "peace agreement" between 1882 and 1888, meeting regularly to discuss and sort out any issues that arose. It did not always work. A 'Forth Bridge' was built, 533 yards long, well upstream at Alloa, by the Caledonian to tap the area's industrial traffic, and also pushing a toe-hold into the North British monopoly of the Clackmannan and Fife coalfields. Inter-company tussling soon began, and the North British successfully fought off a Caledonian effort to get an Alloa-Kirkcaldy line in 1883.

With the coal trade booming, numerous new railways were built in west Lanarkshire to ease congestion and shorten certain routes. In mid-decade the G&SWR monopoly of Ardrossan, flourishing as a coal port, was destroyed by a new company, the Lanarkshire & Ayrshire Railway, whose line diverged from the Caledonian's Beith branch to pass through G&SW territory to a second terminus at Ardrossan Harbour. The CR put up £150,000 of its capital. The line provided a western outlet for Lanarkshire coal, but could easily have joined the Glasgow & South Western at Kilwinning, avoiding a duplication of goods and passenger services between there and Ardrossan.

Having had to live through the 1870s on a very tight-belted regime, the Great North of Scotland Railway was an easy mark for humorists. The tale was told of an American making his first trip on the line. Unimpresssed by the speed of the train, he said to the guard, "Hey, could I get out and pick a few flowers alongside the track?" The guard replied, "There's nae floo'ers to pick." "That's all right," said the visitor. "I've got a packet of seeds with me." But the company took on a new vigour from 1880 with the appointment of an Englishman, William Moffatt, as general manager. He and the chairman, William Ferguson, embarked on expansion, with a line along the coast from Portsoy to Elgin providing a third route from the latter town towards Aberdeen, opened in spring 1884. An Aberdeen suburban service was introduced, and it was a decade of relative harmony with the Highland Railway, resulting in through carriages running between Aberdeen and Inverness. The Great North also introduced a valuable technical innovation in 1889, the automatic tablet exchanger, enabling trains to move from section to section of single track without having to slow down.

Exchange of tokens for single line working, in the 1950s. The signalman hands over a token-pouch with a hoop for manual exchange, and receives a pouch normally used with the automatic tablet exchanger, seen beside his platform. (Stenlake Collection)

An August influx of visitors from the south was a regular annual occurrence, and in 1888 and again in 1895 there were brief phases of open racing between the East and West Coast routes. In 1888 the race was between the day trains from London to Edinburgh, with the East Coast's best time being 7 hours 27 minutes, and the West Coast's 7 hours and 38 minutes. These one-off timings were not maintained and the East Coast standard lapsed back to 8 hours 15 minutes, with the West Coast taking 8 hours 30 minutes. In 1895 competition

Late-Victorian tourism: a 4-horse brake is ready to leave the station at Callande. (Stenlake Collection)

centred on the night trains to Aberdeen, with the East Coast now using the Forth Bridge. Its best timing was 8 hours 40 minutes, just trumped by the West Coast's record of 8 hours 32 minutes. Once again timings reverted by agreement to 10 hours 20 minutes by the East Coast, and 11 hours by the West Coast. The episode showed the rather staid railway companies in unusual sporting mode, but after all, no-one actually wanted to arrive in Aberdeen at five o'clock in the morning.

Cheap Trains and the Goods Rates Crisis

Constant pressure from customer groups ensured that the Government did not let up on its restrictions on railway rates and fares. In 1883 a new Cheap Trains Act updated the 'Gladstone Act' of 1844, exempting the passenger duty from all fares not exceeding one penny a mile and reducing it to 2% on trains at over 1d a mile in urban districts (centres of 100,000-plus, with radius of 12 miles). In return the railways had to make satisfactory (to the Board of Trade) provision of workmen's trains, enabling industrial workers to commute cheaply in large numbers to and from factory districts. The Caledonian was running about 100 such trains daily by 1899, and the G&SWR had 124. Giving evidence to a Parliamentary Select Committee in 1905, the Caledonian's general manager denied that the services were dirty, overcrowded and not as cheap as they could be. The carriages were swept out daily and washed weekly or fortnightly, "depending on the class of men who used them" and the carriages were mostly old oil-lit six-wheelers. The North British had 205 workmen's carriages including eight first class, for foremen, and it also provided women-only compartments. Glasgow was unusual in that the traffic flow of these trains was mostly outwards and in again, reflecting the spread of industry on the city's flanks and the densely-populated central area. Many workmen's halts were makeshift affairs, but in Clydebank Kilbowie Station was resited and a new station named Singer, with three terminal platforms, was opened in 1907 to serve the huge Singer sewing machine factory. Ayrshire had numerous workers' services to collieries and even quiet Annan had one to the tile works at Newbie.

The need for workmen's trains underlined how factories were mass-producing an ever-wider range of goods, with manufacturers and traders soaring in number through the 1880s. While passenger fares were fixed at the lower end by Gladstone's Act and the Cheap Trains Act, the arrangement for goods carriage was quite different. Each company set out its maximum rates for carrying different classes of goods, based on the value per ton, so that a ton of coal would be transported much more cheaply per mile than a hundredweight of fresh-caught salmon. In addition the companies charged 'terminals', extra sums for loading, unloading, storage and delivery. Maximum rates were rarely applied. Large consignors were able to negotiate 'exceptional' rates and every goods manager operated discounts or rebates, known as 'drawbacks', dependent on the volume of traffic provided.

A Parliamentary Select Committee examined railway freight rates and charges in 1881-82, and the Railway Companies' Association (all five Scottish companies were members) had some success in insisting that public interest was their main consideration in fixing rates. Attacks on the charges from the traders' side were poorly co-ordinated. They learned to become a far more effective pressure group and a new campaign was mounted, resulting in the Railway & Canal Traffic Act of 1888, which effectively put railway charges directly under government control. The companies were given six months to submit a revised classification of merchandise traffic to the Board of Trade, and list the maximum rates and charges to be applied. The Board would publish these, consider objections, negotiate alterations, and if necessary impose changes. A massive task for the railway goods departments and for the Board of Trade resulted. When published, the proposed rates caused a storm of protest from individual traders and a range of chambers of ccommerce, agricultural societies and hastily-formed local groups like the Aberdeen, Banff & Kincardine Railway Traders' Defence Association and the Alloa Brewers' Association – 335 combined to form a 'Scottish Objectors' Committee'. Against this vociferous background, it took until 1892 for the review process to produce a new set of maximum rates, fixed by the Board of Trade. Till now it had been the normal practice of railways to charge 'exceptional' rates for around 75% of their goods traffic. Now, claiming they had not had time to devise a scale of exceptional rates

Britain's northernmost junction, Georgemas. The Thurso branch engine is at the water tower. (Stenlake Collection)

below the new maxima, they simply charged most traffic at the top rates. Though perfectly legal this unsurprisingly caused an even greater burst of outrage from the traders. Yet another Parliamentary committee blamed the railway companies for unreasonably disturbing the trade of the country, as if the mess had not been caused by Parliament's own actions; and another Railway & Canal Traffic Act was put together in 1894. It made it obligatory for a railway company to prove that any increase on the rate prevailing on 31 December 1892, if challenged by a customer, was "reasonable" – even if it was below the set maximum. Given the way the companies' charging systems worked, providing proof of reasonability for any specific increase was all but impossible, and the effect was to freeze charges at the December 1892 level. In the expansive economic climate of the 1890s, with traffic rising, this did not seem a grave impediment, but the Acts of 1889-94 had a wholly negative impact on the railways in the 20th century, and mark the demise of the old "railway interest" in the face of newer and more strident lobbying forces.

The companies had played their hand badly: they had become too rigid and complacent, too managerial perhaps in accepting that their 'service' role should compel them to sacrifice their profitability to that of their customers. Transport of freight was the main source of their income, and to cede almost all control over rates and charges was to leave themselves helpless in changing circumstances. Most railway directors were also involved in other businesses, agricultural, industrial or commercial, yet the scale of opposition took them by surprise. Perhaps the traders saw fine stations, huge depots and grand hotels and thought they were subsidising these expensive items. Showiness was part of the culture of the time, as Glasgow's late Victorian industrial architecture still bears witness, and the same people would have criticised the railways for a failure to live up to the imperial spirit. The railway directors might have felt the curse of Calvinism had fallen on them: you're damned if you do, and damned if you don't. Through the 1880s they had spent heavily on improvement: continuous brakes, foot-bridges, station facilities, signalling, corridor carriages with steam heating, with the ratio of expenditure against revenue steadily rising – and a modest increase in carriage rates was greeted as though it were the knell of commercial doom.

The Prime Minister in 1892-94 was Gladstone, leading a minority administration. Fifty years before, he had tried and failed to impose control on railway expansion. Now in its determination to placate the railways' customers, the government prevented the railways from being a dynamic factor in economic life and crippled their freedom of action just as their monopoly-era was coming to an end.

Motive Power and Rolling Stock, 1870-90

Carriage design developed more quickly than that of wagons, with the old four-wheeler, still showing its stage-coach ancestry, superseded by longer six-wheeled vehicles. Larger numbers of travellers required more accommodation, hence the need for longer carriages and also longer trains. Of course this meant heavier trains, requiring greater locomotive power. In 1876 Scottish passengers could experience the smoothness of travel in a bogie carriage for the first time, if they could afford to take the American-style Pullman cars from St. Enoch to St. Pancras. Soon the older rival routes matched the upstarts. From August 1878 two Pullman saloons were added to the East Coast Joint Stock running between London, Edinburgh and Glasgow, and in the following year the North British, South Western and Midland companies combined to operate the Midland Scottish Joint Stock, between St. Pancras, Edinburgh Princes Street (via Carlisle) and St. Enoch. In July 1873 the North British ran the first sleeping car in regular service, with first and second class compartments whose seats converted to beds, and a central lavatory. Usage at first was very low, but soon demand exceeded supply.

A typical third class carriage of the mid-1860s seated 50 people in five compartments, and weighed $7\frac{1}{2}$ tons, requiring the engine to pull 336lbs for every passenger. By the 1890s a third class carriage, with a side corridor and toilet at each end, held 56 passengers in seven compartments, and weighed $29\frac{1}{2}$ tons, or 1,180 lbs per passenger. A great deal more energy was being consumed to carry only a few more fare-paying passengers, and each new generation of carriage was more expensive to build. Greater length required the extension of platforms and the rebuilding of carriage sheds, and their higher level of technical equipment, with gas or electric lighting, running water, automatic brakes and (just coming in at the end of the 19th century) steam heating, meant more frequent and expensive maintenance. It is little wonder that the railways found their working expenses rising inexorably.

The mechanical engineers rose to the challenge of heavier trains. From 1871 the North British pioneered what was to become a standard Scottish type, the inside-cylinder 4-4-0 locomotive, produced by all the companies (except the Highland, which preferred outside cylinders) in models of increasing tractive power over the next forty years, providing the main power of most express and semi-fast services. The most numerous locomotive type was the 0-6-0, again produced in successively more powerful versions by every company, except the Great North, from the 1850s to the early 1920s, working every type of train but with freight overwhelmingly predominating. Tank engines for branch and suburban working were also built in large numbers. Provision of continuous brakes on passenger carriages, either air or vacuum-powered, was completed in the 1890s. On Scottish lines, however, especially the Highland Railway, numerous mixed freight and passenger trains were run, for reasons of economy. To ease shunting of wagons at intermediate stations, passenger carriages were marshalled behind the goods trucks, with no possibility of automatic braking if they became detached. In 1889 a Regulation of Railways Act terminated this practice, and the HR was given three years to comply. It took until November 1897 to do so, and only after some narrow escapes from potentially serious accidents.

Shunters stand to attention with their poles. Also posing are two of Dugald Drummond's standard Caledonian 0-6-0 goods engines. No. 306 ran from 1883 to 1961 (BR 57244) and No. 551 (BR 57340) from 1892 to 1962. (Stenlake Collection)

Last Years of the Monopoly Era – 1890-1899

The Forth Bridge

Already one of the wonders of the modern world, the Forth Bridge was opened on 4 March 1890, a great boost to the prestige of the North British and indeed of Scotland, though the real credit was Matthew Thompson's (since 1883 chairman of the G&SWR as well as of the Midland). With the bridge and a new line from Kinross via Glenfarg, the distance by rail from Edinburgh to Perth was cut by 22 miles, and Edinburgh-Dundee via both bridges by 32. Caledonian services from Princes Street via Stirling suffered accordingly.

Thompson seems to have had a strategic plan. In September 1889 the South Western and the North British had announced that they proposed to amalgamate in August 1890, taking everyone by surprise, not least the Caledonian, whose directors were angered by the South Western's move to ally itself with what they considered a hostile company. It also seemed a departure from the South Western's company's close relationship with the Midland Railway, but Thompson claimed to have suggested the merger. The Midland was sending trains over the NB line from Carlisle to Edinburgh, and was the biggest investor in the Forth Bridge: its strategists in Derby might have foreseen an ultimate take-over of the merged South Western and North British. It was not to be, however. In August 1890 the House of Lords rejected the amalgamation, and an attempt to reintroduce the Bill in 1891 was voted down by South Western shareholders. Though the North British and the North Eastern Railways indulged in some flirtation, the Big Five would remain Scottish until 1923.

LNER Class D49 4-4-0 No 246 *Morayshire* crossing the Forth Bridge on 20 August 1937. The leading vehicle is a horse box. Built in 1928, and later BR No 62712, this engine is preserved on the Bo'ness and Kinneil Railway. (John Alsop Collection)

The 'Scotch Strike'

Railway workers' long-standing grievances about excessive hours without overtime pay had been ignored by the companies, particularly the North British and Caledonian, and trouble was boiling up. The Amalgamated Society of Railway Servants (Scotland) had around 7,000 members by 1890. Still concerned about the dangers of over-long shifts, the government had passed a new Regulation of Railways Act in 1889, requiring companies to record overtime working, but it was a toothless measure, leaving the definition of overtime to the companies. None of the companies would deal with the union. On 21 December 1890 a mass meeting at Glasgow voted for immediate action, and the strike began that day. The Caledonian and North British were most affected, and on the two northern companies there was no strike action. The companies' response was truculent. Strikers were dismissed and threatened with prosecution for breach of their work contracts. Drivers and other workers were recruited from England and Ireland. Bitterness erupted into violence at Motherwell, where the Caledonian had begun proceedings to evict strikers from company-owned houses, and riots broke out on 4 and 5 January 1891. Police and soldiers were brought in and the town's station was damaged by stone-throwing and fighting. Train services were disrupted and much of industry brought to a halt. Coal prices shot up. Public opinion was largely on the railwaymen's side, but the companies refused to negotiate and the North British attempted to sue the union for £20,000. Deadlock went on through January but men gradually drifted back to work, and by the end of the month the strike was effectively over. On the face of it, the strikers had lost, with the companies conceding nothing, but the confrontation marked a change. The railwaymen had shown that they had the power to disrupt industrial and commercial life. They had found political support from the newly-formed Scottish Labour Party. If the companies had won the fight they had lost the argument (and a month's revenue), and the government set up a select committee to inquire into railway servants' working hours. In the end the House of Commons, despite ample evidence of work shifts exceeding twelve hours, decided to exercise only moral pressure on the railway companies to do something about it. This suited the companies very well and they did very little, though they had to publish figures to show instances of excessive hours.

Going Underground in Glasgow

Factory development had spread along the north bank of the Clyde through the 1870s, and Queen's Dock (now the site of the Scottish Exhibition Centre) had opened in 1877. The North British completed a line from Maryhill, on the Queen Street-Helensburgh line, to Stobcross and the NBR-worked Whiteinch Railway from October 1874, and opened the Glasgow, Yoker & Clydebank Railway along the north bank of the Clyde in 1882. In March 1886 an ambitious scheme for a cross-city underground line going east from Stobcross via a low-level station at Queen Street was completed as the Glasgow City & District Railway. The North British took it over in July 1887 and also opened a West End terminus at Hyndland, with trains to Edinburgh via Queen Street (Low Level). Although unpleasant to traverse, always full of smoke (and the scene of some bad accidents as a result) the line substantially eased cross-city traffic. Another underground cross-city line, the Glasgow Central Railway, was built between 1888 and 1896, with stations below street level including Central Station (Low Level). In the 1890s, while it was still being made, the Caledonian took over the company. By the late 1890s Central Station was again overwhelmed, with over 23 million passenger journeys in 1899, and a large-scale rebuilding programme began. From December 1896 Glasgow also had Britain's second underground railway, when the cable-hauled Glasgow District Subway opened.

To cope with Glasgow's ever-increasing goods traffic, the companies added to the goods depots at the older termini, Bridge Street, South Side, Buchanan Street and Queen Street, with others across the city including a great livestock yard at Stobcross. Finally, two huge multi-storey goods stations, College (1880) and High Street (1907), were built flanking the City Union line. Joint ownership of this line was replaced by a separation, with the South Western owning the line from Pollok Junction to College Junction, and lines to the east of College Junction becoming part of the North British system. Glasgow Town Council unsuccessfully opposed the change: as an all-urban line the City of Glasgow Union Railway was valued for rating purposes at £4413 a mile, and its partition into the two large companies, with their long, low-rated rural lines, meant a large reduction in its contribution to the city coffers.

Subsidised Lines

The government's long-standing policy of not subsidising railways was bent a little in the 1890s. It was explained, or excused, as a special case. The north west had long been a disadvantaged area socially and economically, and after several years' hesitation Lord Rosebery's Liberal government agreed in 1894 to give financial support to the construction of a railway from Fort William to Mallaig, and to an extension of the Skye railway from Strome Ferry to Kyle of Lochalsh. Under North British auspices the West Highland line from Craigendoran Junction to Fort William was already under construction. There had been no rush by the public, in Lochaber or anywhere else, to buy West Highland Railway shares and as construction went on and costs mounted, the North British committed itself to investing more and more. Shareholders became suspicious but Lord Tweeddale, NBR chairman, rather in the style of his predecessor Hodgson, wafted away questions at company meetings by saying the West Highland was "a separate concern". The line opened in August 1894, at a final cost of £1,100,000 apart from rolling stock. The NBR did not spare

A classic West Highland Railway scene: LNER 2-6-0 3442 *The Great Marquess* on a Glasgow express between Glen Orchy and Tyndrum (Upper), in 1938. (North British Railway Study Group)

expense on that, providing a new locomotive class for the line, the 'West Highland Bogie' 4-4-0, and four new trains with extra-large windows to reveal the views of the scenic route.

The Highland Railway opened the ten-mile Kyle extension in October 1897, and the 41-mile Mallaig line followed in April 1901, giving the Western Highlands the three termini, Oban, Mallaig and Kyle of Lochalsh, which still exist today, though without the bleating, bellowing livestock, salt barrels, herring boxes and Gaelic conversation that characterised them in their heyday. In 1902 the Mallaig line's revenue was £8357 and operating costs were £19,358. No-one had expected it to be profitable, and the government paid a 3% dividend on £260,000 worth of its capital cost.

The *Financial Times* called the West Highland Railway "a piece of folly", though suspecting correctly that the North British board's real interest was in a continuation of the railway through the Great Glen, providing a shorter route to Inverness and the further north than the Caledonian/Highland line via Perth and Blair Atholl. The Highland Railway had opposed the West Highland project until a ten-year agreement was made in 1889, that the West Highland would not extend north of Banavie, at the south end of the Caledonian Canal. This pact was broken when both the Highland and North British introduced Bills for a railway from Inverness to meet the West Highland at Spean Bridge, but was patched up again. A new situation arose when independent backers proposed a railway from Spean Bridge to Fort Augustus, at the south end of Loch Ness, and obtained an Act in 1896. Claimed as a "local" line, it was generally assumed to be a first step towards Inverness, with its investors expecting to sell out profitably either to the NBR or the Highland. In 1897 both of these companies, and the Invergarry & Fort Augustus itself, applied for authorisation to build on from Fort Augustus to Inverness. The 'Great Glen War' became a national talking point. All the proposals were refused. The Highland Railway had finally got round to building a direct line between Aviemore and Inverness, promised in 1884, whose opening in November 1898 put paid to any

The Eyemouth branch terminus about 1910, with a mixed train. NBR 0-6-0 No 249 was built in 1887 and withdrawn as LNER 9249 in 1938. (Stenlake Collection)

further attempts by other companies to reach Inverness – even by the Great North, which had tried very hard seven times between 1880 and 1893 to get running rights over the Highland Railway, or to build a second line between Elgin and Inverness.

The 1890s saw numerous other extensions and fillings-in, including the Crieff-Comrie Railway (1893) taken over by the Caledonian in 1898; also on the Caledonian the Forfar-Brechin line (1895) with its branch to Edzell in 1896. Under North British auspices, coastal branches opened to Eyemouth (1891) and Aberlady and Gullane (1898). Urban branches included new passenger termini at Bridgeton Cross (1892) and Victoria Park (Whiteinch) in 1896. The Great North opened a branch from Ellon to Boddam, only two miles south of Peterhead, in 1897. The company's new golfing resort hotel was built on this line at Cruden Bay, with its own electric tramway to the station.

Fife in the 1890s

Ever since John Learmonth's time as chairman the North British had used every legal and financial weapon at its disposal to ensure itself a commanding position in Fife, where the expanding coal industry provided growing revenues. One of the reasons for the NBR pursuing the Forth Bridge project was the fear that another company might pre-empt the scheme and gain access. Between repeated attempts by the Caledonian to get a railway into Fife, and the demands of coalowners for ever-more extensive transport and harbour facilities, the North British could not simply sit back and enjoy its privileged position. New links were built in the coalfield area and the NBR took over Burntisland Docks in 1896. In 1897 it absorbed the Anstruther & St. Andrews Railway, an extension of the Leven & East of Fife, which it had owned since 1877.

More than once the coalowners threatened to build their own independent line to carry coal to the coast. Keeping them on-side was a major task, and none was more difficult than Randolph Wemyss, abrasive and volatile landowner and promoter of the Wemyss & Buckhaven Railway, bought by the NBR in 1889 along with Methil and Leven harbours. By 1893 he and others were hustling the railway company to expand Methil Docks: in ten years Scotland's annual coal exports had risen from 2,531,427 tons to 4,531,384 tons. Dock construction was hugely expensive, took a long time, and well aware that the coal industry was highly influenced by economic dips and rises, the NBR was unwilling to provide expensive capacity that might end up under-used. Wemyss and his demands plagued the company, of which he was a director, for ten years, and remain a telling example of how a rich, selfish, well-placed and thoroughly irresponsible individual could influence the policy of a large corporation. Methil got its No. 3 dock in 1913. The North British survived him, at a price, and kept its Fife monopoly to the end.

Peace Breaks Out – Up to a Point

In the winter of 1891-92 the Caledonian and North British made a serious effort to reduce their long mutual hostility, with an agreement to identify 'competitive' traffic and to share the proceeds above a certain level. At first the South Western was also to be included, but backed out of the negotiations and started to undercut the rates agreed between the other two. From 1 May 1892 the NBR abolished its second class fares and carriages (an indication of how much third class accommodation had improved) and the other companies followed suit – the GNSR of course never had a second class. Co-operation still went only so far – in 1892, when its Glasgow, Yoker & Clydebank line was extended to meet the Dumbarton line at Dalmuir, the North British probably felt secure on the north bank of the Clyde, but support from local industry

The station at Currie, Midlothian, about 1908. (Stenlake Collection)

brought in the Caledonian-backed Lanarkshire & Dumbartonshire Railway, to thread a second line in 1896 among the yards and tracks, closer to the river. The Lanarkshire & Dumbartonshire's ambition to build a second railway up the Vale of Leven, with its big dyeworks, was bought off by making the existing NBR line a joint concern.

Around 1898, the long feud between the two northern companies was at last coming to an end. With brief armistice periods, for forty years the Highland and Great North of Scotland Railways had been locked in mutual hostility and non-co-operation. The Highland, feeling itself threatened, was the greater offender, making connections with Great North trains as inconvenient as possible, and seeking to send all traffic by its own route. By 1886 Elgin had three routes to Aberdeen, by Great North via Dufftown or via Buckie and Portsoy (these lines joining at Cairnie, east of Keith) or by the Highland via Mulben to Keith, the shortest route but not the quickest, since the Great North, after 1880, made a point of very smart and efficient working. By 1898, both companies accepted that co-operation was better than confrontation. The election that year of William Whitelaw, related to the Baird industrial magnates, as a director of the HR (he was also a large shareholder in the GNSR) helped to ease the ancient strains. By 1905 the two companies were actively planning to amalgamate.

Competition from the Roads

Mechanised road traffic long preceded the internal combustion engine. The steam-powered road engine, almost as old as the railway locomotive, though eclipsed by the superior power and speed of wheel on rail, trundled on, and by the 1870s traction engines, able to pull two or more loaded carts, were in use, not only in districts where railways did not reach. In the mid-1890s around 200 road engines were working in Aberdeenshire, more than in any other British county apart from Kent (the GNSR had 100 locomotives at that time). Their weight sometimes broke over-bridges never intended to bear such loads and the railways regarded them as a nuisance rather than as real competition. A serious threat to urban passenger services came with the introduction of tramways. Horse-drawn trams began operation in Glasgow in 1872, in Aberdeen in 1874, and from Stirling to Bridge of Allan in the same year, but the impact did not become really serious until electrification speeded up the tramways from the late 1890s. Railways tried and almost invariably failed to prevent municipalities and private companies from obtaining Acts allowing tramway construction. The Great North of Scotland Railway tried to take over Aberdeen's tramways in 1895, with the forward-looking aim of creating an integrated urban transport system, but the city council opposed it and took over the trams as a municipal enterprise. Extension of electric tram networks drew off much suburban and inter-town traffic. Perth, Kirkcaldy, Falkirk, Dunfermline, Kilmarnock and Ayr all had tramway systems, with Ayr's stretching from Alloway to Prestwick, and Falkirk's to Grangemouth. It was possible to go all the way from Wishaw to Paisley by tram. Against this discouraging background a strange contest took place when the South Western and Caledonian both established suburban railways around Paisley and Barrhead. They shared ownership of the Glasgow-Paisley line and of a new line from Renfrew to meet their joint line at Cardonald, but they opened competing lines from Paisley to Barrhead between 1902 and 1905, just when the Paisley tram network was being extended there. The Caledonian spent £720,000 on developing railways around Paisley, but its new station at Barrhead never saw a train. The South Western's service between Paisley and a new terminus, Barrhead Central, lasted only eight years. Massive arches and earthworks around the town still bear witness to these futile ventures. Perhaps a more valuable exercise by the G&SWR was to build a 12.5 mile duplicate line between Dalry and Johnstone, with Scotland's first flying junction at Brownhill where it diverged from the original line to Ayr. Opened in 1905, it speeded up traffic along the route and gave better railway access to the communities of Kilbarchan, Lochwinnoch and Kilbirnie.

Hotels and Catering

Hotel ownership by the railway companies began as a natural extension of their passenger transport business. The Highland's first precursor, the Inverness & Nairn Railway, was early in action, setting up the Station Hotel at Inverness in 1856. Dumfries Station had hotel rooms in the upper floor from the 1850s, until the present Station Hotel was built in 1897. From 1879 to the early 1900s was the era of the grand railway hotel, with St. Enoch Station Hotel (G&SWR) in 1879, and the Central Hotel (CR, 1883) in Glasgow; the GNSR's take-over of the Palace Hotel in Aberdeen (1890); and the jointly-owned Perth Station Hotel (1890). Edinburgh's North British Hotel, towering above Waverley Station, was opened in 1902, and the Caledonian Hotel, less imposing but equally grand inside, followed in 1903. With the growth of tourism the companies also invested in resort hotels, with the Great North of Scotland leading the way in 1899 at Cruden Bay. The Highland built holiday hotels at Kyle of Lochalsh, Dornoch and Strathpeffer, and the G&SWR opened Turnberry in 1906. Last (until 1986) and grandest was the Caledonian's vast establishment at Gleneagles, whose building was delayed by the 1914-18 war, and when it opened in 1924 the Caledonian no longer existed. The railway hotels were at the top end of the market, and the companies incurred some criticism for not making provision for less well-off travellers, but they were seen as prestige establishments. By 1923 there were seventeen railway hotels, and (Cruden Bay a sad exception) they made a profit.

Each company also operated refreshment rooms, usually on tenancy agreements, at main stations and junctions, segregated into first and third class at larger stations, as well as leasing space for bookstalls, florists, tobacconists and sometimes hairdressers. At bigger stations boys with trays plied the platforms, selling chocolate, fruit and newspapers. Hearing a Forfar lad call out "Forfar rock! World famous!" a travelling youth leaned out and said, "Never heard o't," to which the sales-boy retorted, "It's easy seen *ye* hinna been far."

Traders' Wagons

By the end of 1899 the Scottish railway system had reached 3,485 miles. There were still 26 separate companies but all trains were run by one or other of the Big Five. Now with 2,241 locomotives, 5,270 passenger carriages, 2,184 other passenger vehicles, and 145,604 goods vehicles, in 1899 they provided 122,201,102 passenger journeys, for receipts of £4,540,393; and carried 47,079,707 tons of minerals and 12,273,968 tons of general merchandise, for receipts of £6,258,004. Passenger train miles amounted to 17,153,256, and freight to 17,068,574. In a practice going back to the beginnings of public railways, and still familiar today, regular consignors of wagon-load quantities might own their own wagons, in any number from one or two to several thousand, though (except for short trips between their own sidings in places like Coatbridge) their own locomotives did not run on railway company tracks. The vast majority were owned by coal companies. The railway saved on wagon construction and maintenance, and was less likely to have an excess of its own wagons during slack periods of trade. The system was not without problems: traders' wagons were not always well-maintained and might cause accidents, and a customer with its own wagon fleet was in a stronger position to defect to another line. In 1888 the Scottish Waggon Owners' Association was set up, and by mid-1889 its members had over 24,000 wagons.

In 1909 the Caledonian Railway began a passenger shuttle service over the Connel Bridge using a converted charabanc fitted with railway wheels. A flat truck could be attached to it to take a car, or in this case a motorcycle and sidecar, over the bridge for fifteen shillings. (Stenlake Collection)

Modernise or Economise? – 1900-1914

New Opportunities

The first decade of the 20th century was not an easy time for the railways, with a complete change of mood from the over-confident 1890s. Challenges had to be faced on several fronts. Working costs were rising faster than revenue. New technology was available, with far greater use of electrical power for lighting, communication and signalling, but required substantial investment. Electric traction, already in use on urban and interurban tramway systems, was becoming a serious alternative to steam power. The tenor of industrial relations was changing: at the start of the decade the companies were still obdurate in their refusal to deal with trade unions, but extension of the franchise to all males over 21 and the rise of the Labour Party were putting greater political power in the hands of the working class, and the railway unions steadily gained strength. Motor cars and vans were venturing onto the roads. Turbine steamers were shortening sea-passage times and aviators were making rapid improvements to the original kite-like flying machines. There was much for railway managements to do and to learn.

In many ways the companies responded positively. However, there was one difficulty above all that they had to contend with. The legislation of 1894 had severely hampered their ability to raise fares and charges, and they had to meet the conditions of the 1900s with the financial equivalent of an automatic brake locked to their wheels. An attempt in 1900 by the three southern companies to increase the carriage rate for coal was rejected by the Railway & Canal Commissioners because they could not properly prove the need for it, being unable to supply exact figures of their coal train mileage. Coal prices were rising fast and they were still carrying it at 1892 rates with no serious possibility of an increase. The coalowners were very pleased. For all five companies the great watchword had to be not Modernise! but Economise! With extremely limited opportunities to increase income per train-mile, every aspect of operating costs had to be examined with a view to reduction. New projects had to be justified and costed. The impossibility of enlarging their squeezed profit margins also made it very hard for the companies to raise capital for new projects, as only a minimal return for investors could be guaranteed. Just at a time when major technical improvements had become possible, the railways were starved of investment capital.

The largest projects of the decade were the completion of schemes begun in the more expansive-minded 1890s, like the new locomotive works of the Great North of Scotland Railway at Inverurie, completed in 1902, and built on a scale much greater than was needed, probably with an eye on amalgamation with the Highland Railway, whose works at Inverness were small and old-fashioned. Projects in Glasgow included the enlargement of St. Enoch Station, with a second arched train-shed and a total of twelve platforms, and re-signalling of the approach lines, completed in 1901. Between 1901 and 1906 the Caledonian was also enlarging the nearby Central Station, a project which included a second access bridge over the Clyde. The new Central, designed by James Miller and Donald Matheson, had 14,000 square yards of space compared with 6,250 in the previous station, and its gently sloping concourse and curved building lines made it one of the most sophisticated railway terminals in the world. Glasgow's port facilities were boosted by the Prince's Dock on the south bank, opened in 1900 and served by a joint CR-NBR-G&SWR branch from Ibrox. Seven years later the great Rothesay Dock was opened on the north bank, served by the North British and Lanarkshire & Dumbartonshire lines, diverting much coal traffic from Ardrossan Harbour and from the Glasgow and South Western and Lanarkshire & Ayrshire lines.

Both the CR and NBR were also active in Edinburgh. Princes Street Station burned down in 1903 and was replaced by a new train-shed, fronted by the Caledonian Hotel. The Caledonian also built a line across Leith to the docks in 1902-03, intended for goods and passengers. Stations were built, but a passenger service never materialised. The North British built a large new terminus, Leith Central, in 1903, with links to the main line towards Waverley and Berwick. Like the railways around Paisley, these were late efforts to capture a suburban traffic that was being drawn away by the electric tram (though Edinburgh's slow cable-worked system gave Leith Central's traffic a few years' grace). In Aberdeen the Great North was enlarging the Joint Station in Aberdeen, in stages between 1902 and 1915.

Light Railways and Country Lines

Country branches were still being pushed out. The Lauder and the Gifford & Garvald Light Railways opened in 1901, worked by the North British. The Highland Railway began working the Dornoch Light Railway in 1902 and the Wick & Lybster Light Railway in 1903, the same year as the GNSR opened the Fraserburgh-St. Combs branch and the Callander & Oban its line from Connel Ferry to Ballachulish, with substantial viaducts at the mouth of Loch Etive and across Loch Creran. Slate traffic was hoped for, though the slate quarries continued to send out much of their product by sea. In 1905 the South Western opened the Cairn Valley Light Railway to Moniaive. This flurry of light railway construction was caused by the Light Railways Act of 1896, which offered a considerable easing of the authorisation procedures and also held out the possibility of government grants for light railways that were unlikely to raise local capital. A light railway was subject to specific working conditions including a maximum speed of 25 mph. Many other schemes were proposed under the Light Railways Act but failed to get sufficient financial backing. Far away from the Big Five, a passenger service began in 1905 on the narrow-gauge Campbeltown & Machrihanish Railway in Kintyre, set up in the 1870s to carry coal from the Machrihanish mine (finally closed in 1934).

Campbeltown & Machrihanish Railway at the Quay Head Terminus in Campbeltown. (Stenlake Collection)

A new coast-to-coast route came into existence in 1905 when the Strathearn line, open to St. Fillans in 1901, was extended to a junction at Balquhidder, making it possible to travel by train from Dundee and Perth to Oban via Crieff, though the junction pointed south to Stirling rather than west to Oban. Its promoters optimistically hoped it would 'open up' the country, but its traffic outside the short tourist season was always very small. There was a somewhat stronger economic base for the Caledonian's Lanarkshire line in coal country between Hamilton and Strathaven, opened in 1902-1905, yet this too was built only because the Duke of Portland threatened to make his own railway to carry coal from his mines to the harbour at Troon. The Caledonian in effect did it for him, at its own cost, joining its Lanarkshire network to the Glasgow & South Western at Darvel with a line from Strathaven. In 1906 the North British reluctantly fulfilled a commitment from the previous decade to open a railway between Kincardine and Dunfermline. By the end of 1906 this spurt of railway construction had largely ceased. Most of these late lines had very limited services and some would see early closure.

Co-operation and Competition

In a culmination of their reconciliation, late in 1905 the Great North of Scotland and Highland Railways announced a plan to combine to form the Highland & North of Scotland Railway. The companies, though of very different geographical shape, were otherwise very much of a size and fit. Vehement opposition from many HR shareholders resulted in the Highland's withdrawal from the plan, though co-operation between the two companies remained. This was the last attempt among the five companies to amalgamate with one another. One of the Great North of Scotland's initiatives was to operate buses and lorries in country districts without a railway. By 1913 it owned 35 buses, tying in with train arrivals at key points, and eight goods and parcels lorries, while the other companies had virtually none. It also ran road-rail tours.

A Great North of Scotland Railway bus, around 1908. The vehicle is a 20/25 hp Milnes-Daimler, acquired in 1905 as a lorry. (Stenlake Collection)

In 1905 both the Caledonian and the North British inaugurated luxurious new express trains from Glasgow and Edinburgh to Aberdeen, but by the end of 1907 the imperative need for economies led to a twenty-year agreement for the sharing and rationalisation of competitive services within Scotland. But the habits of a lifetime are not easy to shake off, and in 1909 the NBR was persuaded to back a new line, the Newburgh & North Fife Railway, which offered an alternative route to the Caledonian between Perth and Dundee, via the Tay Bridge. It proved a hopeless loss-maker.

Denied rate increases, and seeking every means of improving efficiency and extracting revenue, the managers of the Caledonian, North British and Glasgow & South Western companies jointly informed their customers that demurrage charges on wagons and tarpaulin sheets would be imposed from 1 August 1908, together with a charge for extended occupancy of company-owned sidings. Demurrage, a charge levied on rolling stock or railway equipment held by a customer for longer than a specified time, had always been provided for in the Acts setting up the railway companies, but had rarely been invoked, and the customers, incensed by the change in policy, refused to pay, taking their case to the Railway & Canal Commissioners. In January 1911 the commissioners ruled in favour of the railways. Wagons began to be returned with remarkable promptitude, making thousands more available at any time. At this time the three southern companies were also discussing the possibility of pooling their wagon stock, and a group of officials was sent to Germany to study its *Wagen-Union* scheme, reporting favourably in May 1911. No action was taken then, but the initiative would pay off in five years' time.

The North British was also under strong pressure from the Lothian coal industry, which had expanded greatly through the 1890s and 1900s while the railway company had resisted its demands for more line capacity. Refused an Act to build their own lines in 1911, the coal-owners re-applied in 1913, finally spurring the NBR to obtain its own 'Lothian Lines' Act and proceed with expansion of the local system. In 1916 its chairman would remark that the extra capacity was providing great value to the coalowners and the Government "at the expense of the NBR deferred shareholders".

The Unions Finally Acknowledged

Constant emphasis in all companies on cost-cutting precluded any pay rise and created a mood of resentment and anger among railway workers. An Amalgamated Society of Railway Servants ballot of members in September 1907 showed 90% in support of strike action. Fearing the consequences of a national strike, the government stepped in and made separate agreements with the companies and the union (the companies would still not talk to the union), which provided for conciliation boards to be set up, with representatives both of management and staff, to deal with questions of pay and working conditions. Six boards in each company were set up to cover the various staff groups from enginemen to permanent way workers and ticket collectors. It was a clever fix, negotiated by David Lloyd George as President of the Board of Trade, but by 1911 the railwaymen were thoroughly disenchanted with the results and a sudden strike was threatened in August. This was at a time of war threat, the 'Moroccan Crisis' confrontation with Imperial Germany, and may have encouraged the government to find a quick solution. Scottish railway workers had a genuine grievance. In 1901 they had numbered 43,710 and their average weekly wages were £1 3s 2d. By 1910 their numbers had increased to 46,105 and though the cost of living had risen during the decade, their average wages had fallen to £1 2s 8½d a week, including overtime pay. In England

Caledonian 4-6-0 No. 903 *Cardean* at Gretna. Built in 1906 and withdrawn in 1930, for years it hauled the 2 pm Glasgow Central-London Euston express. (John Alsop Collection)

and Wales railwaymen were earning a weekly average of £1 6s 3½d in 1910, 13.6% more than their Scottish counterparts.

The Government offered a royal commission to investigate the working of the 1907 scheme, and the companies agreed to accept its findings if the Act of 1894 were amended to allow rate rises to offset any increase in their labour costs. This was agreed. The railway chiefs were learning to be a little more flexible: Sir Charles Bine Renshaw of the Caledonian noted that: "In the great industries such as steel and coal, recognition [of unions] was to a certain extent conceded. It was therefore necessary to indicate the limits wherein recognition was least unsafe." The commission reported in October, recommending a modified conciliation scheme which gave conciliation boards freedom to appoint a secretary "from any source they may think proper" (i.e. including unions). This was not enough for the railwaymen and another strike was threatened. By the end of November recognition of the unions' role in negotiating pay and conditions was conceded. It was noted that "the Scottish companies evinced the greatest suspicion of the entire proceedings, with their suspicion of the Government matched only by their suspicion of each other." In their long refusal to accept union representation the Scottish companies can fairly be accused of undue complacency, even arrogance. David Cooper, general manager of the Glasgow & South Western, was typical in describing his staff as "a most loyal and contented body of men", though they had to battle hard against his resistance to get a modest rise in pay via the conciliation boards in 1912.

The promise to allow rate increases was implemented in the Railway & Canal Traffic Act of 1913. In May that year the railways gave notice of a 4% rise in rates, from 1 July, prompting an outraged reaction from the traders. Yet another royal commission, a "small" one, was set up to report on the relations between railway companies and the state, examining "the extent to which a private industry that had become a public utility ought to be subject to public control". Nationalisation was to be an option (in 1914 the MP Leo Chiozza-Money introduced a railway nationalisation Bill, which got as far as a second reading before events overtook it). The Railway Companies' Association did not object to nationalisation, so long as the terms were at least as favourable as those set out in the Act of 1844. War was to intervene before this issue – which should have been properly faced 70 years before – could be followed up, and the commission was abandoned.

As the last full year of peace, 1913 was significant, since its operating and financial results would be used as a benchmark for calculating company earnings during the seven years of government control which started in August 1914. The results were helped by a strong economic background in the year when Scottish coal production reached its maximum level, at 42.5 million tons. Total passenger journeys were 130,659,926, apart from those made by 71,000 season ticket holders; and passenger receipts, with mails and parcels, came to £5,635,012. General merchandise accounted for 15,919,725 tons, coal for 43,302,287 tons, and other minerals for 14,480,176 tons, with a total revenue of £7,787,0771, of which general merchandise accounted for £4,383,783 and coal for £2,539,024. A total of 1,196,677 cattle were carried, and 4,345,533 sheep.

The route mileage was 3,684, and engines numbered 2,819. Passenger trains ran 28,5117,622 miles and freight 19,551,861 miles. Total engine mileage in the year was calculated at 77,613,875 (the difference comes from empty stock workings, shunting, etc.) – it looks a huge amount, but means an average of some 530 miles per engine per week. The companies had 6,885 passenger carriages (335,916 seats) and 3,152 other passenger-train vehicles. Goods vehicles totalled 137,439 plus 6,882 service vehicles. The companies' combined gross income was £13,602,194, and after deduction of the working expenses, their net income was £6,258,588, of which £4,118,971 was paid in dividends to shareholders. Including debentures and loans, the authorised capital value of Scottish railways was £167,916,443, though the total amount raised and ranking for dividend on 31 December 1913 was £179,205,342.

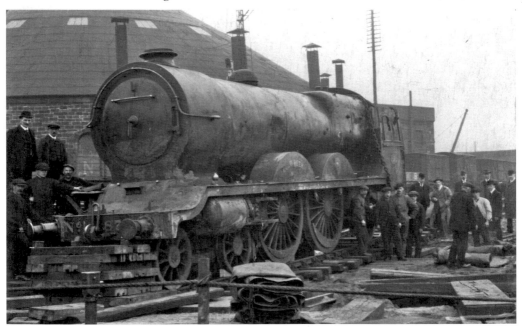

On 14 April 1914 NBR Atlantic No. 872 *Auld Reekie* collided with a shunting goods train at Burntisland Station. Two people were killed. Here the damaged locomotive has been re-railed. To the left is the locomotive roundhouse, built c1847, demolished in 1935. (Stenlake Collection)

World War I and the Grouping

State Control

Back in 1871 an Act for the Regulation of the Railways had made provision for immediate state control of any railway company, or all companies, in an emergency – yet another indication that railways were a fundamental part of national infrastructure. The companies were used to moving large bodies of troops and had already worked out draft plans for full-scale mobilisation. All five moved slickly into action as soon as war was declared on 4 August 1914. With all other railways in Great Britain they were placed under the control of the new Railway Executive Committee. A complicated system of remuneration was imposed. All government traffic was to be carried without charge. All receipts would be passed to the government which would repay the companies according to their net earnings and expenditures in 1913 (and retain any surplus). A later amendment provided that the government would pay 4% interest on account of any new investments and capital expenditure made by the companies since the war began. The company boards and managements remained in place but the Executive was in ultimate control. Its eleven members were all railway managers, only one of them, Donald Matheson of the Caledonian, from a Scottish company. The North British, with its Edinburgh HQ near to the Army's Scottish Command, was designated "secretary company" to liaise with the military authorities.

The Greatest Disaster

Once it became clear the conflict would not be a short one, the steady build-up of the war effort ensured that the railways would be intensely busy, despite reductions to normal services. Wartime traffic was involved in the catastrophic accident at Quintinshill, on the Caledonian main line just north of Gretna, in the early morning of 22 May 1915, when a southbound troop train crashed head-on into a northbound local train, which had been placed on the same line to allow the late-running north-bound overnight express to overtake it. Almost immediately this third train ploughed into the wreckage. A vast mound of burning, shattered carriages covered all the tracks. It remains the worst railway disaster in British history, with 227 killed and another 246 injured, many of them badly burned. The inquiry revealed a deplorable state of negligence and casual attitudes to the regulations at the Quintinshill signal box, and the signalman was jailed for culpable homicide.

Wartime Working

On the North British, an initiative begun before the war proved valuable during the years of conflict. In 1914 the company introduced a control system with a central office and district offices (Eastern, Monklands & Western, Fife & Northern) controlling all goods train movements and deploying wagons and locomotives with the aim of eliminating all unnecessary running. All engines carried head-codes and their numbers were painted on the tenders for quick recognition. Telephone and telegraph linked all signal boxes to the control offices. The need to maximise the use of all goods vehicles also speeded up the moves towards wagon-pooling and from 5 June 1916 the North British, Caledonian and Glasgow & South Western began a pooling scheme that covered 103,366 wagons, which was joined by the Highland and Great North from January 1917. A central wagon office was established in the NBR's Glasgow offices. Traders' wagons, very numerous, remained outside the pool, though railway companies were allowed to put loads into traders' wagons that might otherwise be returned empty.

A scene from 1914-15, with a large crowd gathered at Wick Station to see off Territorial Army troops, bound for the Western Front. (Stenlake Collection)

An armoured train with a 12-pounder gun and Maxim machine-guns patrolled the Forth Bridge. The Caledonian and North British each supplied 25 engines for service in France, and the hard-pressed Highland was lent seven Caledonian and two North British engines as well as several from English companies. Railways played an important part in the installation and work of the 'national factories' set up in 1916-17 at various places to manufacture munitions on a huge scale. The largest stretched almost all the way from Gretna to Annan; another was set up at Bishopton in Renfrewshire. They had their own stations and scheduled workers' train services to tie in with work shifts. Arrivals and departures at Gretna Station, totalling 10,747 in 1913, reached 2,932,814 in the peak year of 1917. Women workers in these factories far outnumbered men.

Duplicated services were heavily cut back from 1 January 1917, with 47 Caledonian stations closed, all in places where an alternative company's service was available. Lines in the north were far busier than in peacetime and some duplication, as between Aviemore and Inverness, was valuable. But the Highland's line between Keith and Portessie was closed and the rails lifted for use on new Admiralty lines around Invergordon. Another victim of wartime economy was the venerable horse-hauled Inchture Tramway on the Perth-Dundee line, opened in 1848 and closed on 1 January 1917. Railway steamer services were drastically curtailed, with most ships taken over by the Admiralty and converted to minesweepers or troop transports, and all the resort hotels, except for Cruden Bay, were taken over for use as hospitals, training schools or recuperation centres.

To speed up wartime supply trains, new crossing loops were added on the long single-track lines, and new access lines were laid to some airfields like Lenabo in Aberdeenshire and Donibristle in Fife. In Easter Ross a new railway was laid parallel to the existing line between Alness and Invergordon to serve the naval base, mainly for carrying mines, and the Dingwall-Kyle line was taken over completely by the Admiralty for the transport of American-made mines. Another mine depot was set up at Inverness, with a new connection and sidings by the Caledonian Canal at Muirtown. A new branch was laid from Inverkeithing to the naval yard at Rosyth. With Britain's Grand Fleet based at Scapa Flow, the east coast ports were intensely busy with naval supplies. Steam coal came from South Wales to Grangemouth in 'Jellicoe Specials' named after the admiral in command. Most other naval supplies went from Aberdeen (where the GNSR had made the timely acquisition of shunting engines to replace horses at the harbour). Mails and many other items were taken along the Highland's 280 miles between Stanley Junction and Thurso, as well as thousands of men who endured the 'Misery' naval train which took 21½ hours from Euston to the northern terminus.

War Wages and Women Workers

For Scottish railway workers, the wartime organisation of railways as a single national service meant an important and welcome change – pay rates were equalised across all British railway companies. Scottish pay rates (like Scottish fares and goods charges) had always been lower than in England. Deep disapproval was expressed by the five companies, who said it must be regarded only as a temporary wartime measure. In the course of the war years the cost of living doubled, with all sorts of goods and commodities rising steeply in cost, and the pay of railway workers had to be regularly supplemented by "war wages" additions. The companies' wage bill mounted hugely, but no increase in rates and charges was allowed until January 1917 when reduced-price tickets were abolished, except for workmen's and season tickets, and normal fares increased by 50%.

Hardly any war damage as a result of enemy action occurred on the railways, but intensive use of locomotives and rolling stock, shortage of technical staff, use of railway workshops for the production of military equipment, and very little in the way of new engines and wagons, all meant that the condition of railway equipment gradually deteriorated. Make-do-and-mend was increasingly practised, and the size of the post-war repair and replacement bill got steadily larger.

A remarkable aspect of the railways' vital contribution to building up and maintaining such a high level of activity in the national war effort was that they accomplished it despite losing a substantial proportion of their workers to the armed forces. Railwaymen were exempted when conscription was introduced, but almost a quarter of the Scottish railwaymen had joined up, and 1,957 were killed on active service. To an extent the volunteers were replaced by new employees, often women: by 1918 around 4,800 women were employed, more than three times the pre-war number, primarily as clerks, cleaners and porters. Train crews and signalmen worked long-extended shifts to keep traffic rolling. The achievement is worthy of notice. An efficiency-minded person might suspect previous over-manning, but the response to a sustained national crisis cannot be compared to normal conditions.

A New Dispensation: the Grouping

At the inevitable cost of inconvenience to the travelling public, the railways' part in the war effort was generally acknowledged. The war years also made it apparent that it was very much in the national interest to treat railways as one basic British system. Though there were only five companies (always excepting the isolated Campbeltown & Machrihanish and the Glasgow Subway) running trains in Scotland, there were around 95 in England and Wales, and the necessity for rationalisation was much more strongly felt south of the Border. Even in Scotland, though the companies were not run-down to the point of exhaustion, a return to the quintuple set-up of boards, managements, and workshops seemed no way to achieve a railway fit for the 20th century, and it was generally accepted that a reorganisation was necessary. Once again, the vital place of railways within the economic framework made government action inevitable: there was no question of simply paying off the companies for their wartime service and leaving them to sort themselves out in a new way. There was to be an imposed solution. Its architect was Sir Eric Geddes, a forceful and determined figure, born in India to a Scots-colonial family, once deputy general manager of the North Eastern Railway, who had earned a wartime reputation for getting things done. The government flirted with the idea of state ownership but recoiled from the commitment to modernise the infrastructure of such a vast industry. Instead Geddes devised a 'grouping' into a small number of very large companies, which would remain as independent organisations owned by their shareholders, but would operate under conditions set out and maintained by the government. The Ministry of Transport was set up, under Geddes, in 1919 to provide governance of all transport, rail, road, sea and air, with far more power than the Board of Trade had possessed.

Following a wartime promise, from 1 February 1919, despite strong objections from all railway companies, an eight-hour working day was conceded to all grades of railway staff. With the government-supported wartime pay scheme due to end, the companies were determined to enforce pay cuts, and a national railway strike was called for 26 September that year. It lasted until 5 October and for the first time all five companies were involved. Even on the Highland and Great North of Scotland, the old tradition of company loyalty and 'family spirit' was gone. The era of deference was over. A settlement extended the war-wage package for another year.

Several possible combinations of the railway companies were considered, including a separate Scottish group, formed either by the Great North joining the North British, with the other three forming a second company; or a single group bringing all five together. Both proposals were opposed by the managements of the Scottish companies, who preferred the option of merging with one or other of the English groups. Scottish railway workers, afraid of cuts in pay and conditions in an all-Scottish system, also preferred the idea of cross-Border mergers, as did commercial and industrial customers, who feared rates and charges would go up. After much pressure from Scotland, Geddes accepted that the Great North of Scotland and North British Railways should become part of the Eastern group, and the Highland, Caledonian and Glasgow & South Western should be amalgamated into the Midland and London & North Western group. As the London & North Eastern (LNER) and the London, Midland & Scottish (LMS) Railways, the new companies went live on 1 January 1923.

This massive change, and all the necessary negotiation and preparation, went in parallel with the resolution of another complicated issue, centred on the termination of the wartime control system, and the railway companies' claims against the government. The 1871 Act required the state to hand the railways back to their owners in the same condition as when they had been taken over. After the years of intensive usage and patched-up maintenance since 1914, this was a huge obligation, estimated to cost up to £150 million. In a political masterstroke, the government combined the two issues of amalgamation and compensation. It was made obligatory for the companies, in agreeing the amalgamations, to accept and share a total amount of £60 million as full payment for all wartime wear and tear.

Ordnance QF 18-pounder field gun carriages in storage at one of William Beardmore's works, probably Dalmuir, during the First World War. After 1920 the company built locomotives at their Dalmuir Works supplying the LNER, LMS and overseas railways. (Stenlake Collection)

Of this sum the Scottish companies received £6,215,000, or just over 10%. The North British engaged in a protracted legal dispute with the Ministry of Transport over its claims for compensation during the control period, which the Ministry considered excessively high. In the end a compromise was reached, in which the North British reduced its claim somewhat, but achieved a moral victory.

The Railways Act of 1921 set out the final form of the amalgamations and defined the Ministry of Transport's powers of regulation and supervision. The new giant companies were not to be masters in their own domains. A Railways Rates Tribunal was set up to control rates and charges, with the aim of yielding a "standard net revenue" equivalent to that which the constituent companies had earned in 1913; and a National Wages Board to rule on pay matters. Government control of the railways through the Railway Executive ended on 15 August 1921, and four days later the provisions of the Railways Act came into force.

So Scotland's Big Five vanished from the scene, though it took several years before the re-branding of stations, uniforms, rolling-stock and all the hundreds of items of equipment was complete. Their legacy was a complete railway system, indeed over-complete in some areas, with all its installations. How far the expansion of the railways led or nourished economic and industrial development has been much debated, with recent economic historians tending to play down the railways' significance. It is certainly true that the railways, at least from the 1850s on, were as much the product of commercial and industrial development as generators. Yet their social and communal impact was revolutionary in a great variety of ways, transforming social mobility, improving living standards, widening the opportunities for local commerce, expanding tourism, and bringing a far stronger sense of national communication and integration than had existed before. Traditionalists, and the minority of people at the time who felt that Scottish institutions should be run in Scotland, regretted the companies' demise. Whatever the view of their efficiency and quality, they were based, managed, and largely owned in Scotland and could be held accountable at annual meetings. The chairmen and directors were known and visible. Scotland was their territory and they had a vested interest in providing the country with a service which offered some cause for satisfaction, even pride. Each company had a strong sense of identity and of its own history, which percolated among the 50,000-plus railway workers. Tales of rivalry, like those of Caledonian and Glasgow & South Western drivers racing each other on the almost-parallel lines past Ardeer, or the North British and Caley battling to be first at Kinnaber Junction in the 'Race to the North', or Highland porters at Elgin carefully re-labelling parcels meant to be forwarded via the Great North of Scotland, are enshrined in railway folklore and reminiscence. The travelling public as a whole was largely indifferent: so long as a railway service was there, they did not mind who provided it.

Motive Power and Rolling Stock, 1890-1923

For a few years in the 1890s, Scotland seemed to be a leader in British locomotive development. In 1894 the Highland's locomotive superintendent, David Jones, introduced the first 4-6-0 engine for home use, and this new step-up in power was followed by 4-6-0s for express work on the Caledonian and Glasgow & South Western. At the same time, the Caledonian's chief mechanical engineer, J.F. McIntosh, extended the power of the traditional 4-4-0 with his 'Dunalastair' series by enlarging the boiler and fire space. By the 1900s Scottish design (apart from export production from the North British Locomotive Co. in Glasgow) was no longer in the front rank, constrained by limited resources and old-fashioned equipment and techniques. For its expresses the North British opted from 1906 for 4-4-2 'Atlantics', like its East Coast associates to the south. The Great North of Scotland was unique in having no 0-6-0 tender locomotives, using 4-4-0s for all types of main line services. Superheating, developed in Germany, was applied to some new engines from 1911, increasing their tractive power. To the end, the five companies produced their own locomotive types. No-one ever seems to have suggested that collaboration here would have been a huge saving. But using whose designs?

From 1890, gangway connections between corridor carriages appeared on some English lines but were not seen on Scottish railways until the North British and Caledonian, vying for custom on the Aberdeen route, introduced complete new trains in the mid-1900s. Carriages could have a thirty-year life-span, and each company's stock ranged from elderly, oil-lit, unheated, non-corridor six-wheelers to up-to-date, electrically-lit, steam-heated bogie coaches, making the travel experience on the Black Isle line, for example, very different to that on the main lines. The twisty Balerno branch had new four-wheel coaches with electric light built for it in 1921.

Shipping Services

Space does not allow for more than a mention of the railways' shipping interests, which were also transferred with the amalgamations. These began from an early stage with the Ayrshire line. The Firth of Clyde was the main arena, with the G&SW, Caledonian and North British all operating steamer fleets, often in competition. The North British also had ships in the Firth of Forth, the South Western ran the Stranraer-Larne service, and the Highland did likewise for a time between Scrabster and Stromness. The Forth, Tay and Kyke-Kyleakin ferries were run by the railways, and railway or railway-backed vessels also operated on Loch Lomond, Loch Tay and Loch Awe, and along the Caledonian Canal.

The Big Two

Two Ways of Running a Railway

On 1 January 1923, the same men and women worked in the same stations, and the same engines pulled the same carriages, but everyone was braced for change. The two new companies were huge and remote. Their headquarters were in London, their main operational bases were Derby, Crewe and Horwich for the LMS, and Doncaster and Darlington for the LNER, and Scotland for both was one of several divisional areas, accounting for approximately one seventh of their total activity. There was no sudden change, since management and service down to station level had be maintained, but it soon became clear that the companies had adopted different strategies for running their conglomerate empires. On the LMS, there was a strong trend towards centralisation of control, while the LNER adopted a more devolved approach. The LNER, however, was an assemblage of companies that had long co-operated, certainly as far as the North British and North Eastern (on the whole) were concerned, and if the North British had had little to do in the past with the Great North, at least they had not been enemies; while the LMS was composed largely of former rivals. The Caledonian and the Highland were old allies but that could not be said of the Caledonian and the Glasgow & South Western. Both Groupings set up advisory committees for their Scottish areas and for some years each area was subdivided into northern and southern sections, the northern ones being the former Highland and Great North of Scotland systems.

To the LMS, Scotland was the Northern Division, headed until 1927 by Donald Matheson of the Caledonian, as deputy general manager (Scotland) – a post abolished with his retirement. The LNER's more lateral arrangement was based on the old constituent companies. James Calder, former general manager of the North British,

The archway in the Inverness locomotive yard held water tanks. It was demolished in 1961. 'Jones Goods' No. 115, LMS No. 17928, built in 1894, was withdrawn in 1933. On the incline behind them are former Glasgow & South Western Railway coal wagons. (Stenlake Collection)

was appointed general manager (Scotland) with considerable latitude on train operations, locomotive running, signalling, engineering work, property dealing, steamers and hotels. His ex-boss, North British chairman William Whitelaw, elected as chairman of the LNER, was also his new boss, and Whitelaw's regular presence at the Scottish board showed a greater awareness of, and sensitivity to, the particular needs and requirements of the company's Scottish lines than the LMS displayed. On the LMS, the larger of the two corporations, pulling things together was begun under the chairmanship of Sir Guy Granet of the Midland Railway, who set up a vertical-type management structure with departmental chiefs at HQ controlling most functions. This intensified with the arrival of Sir Josiah

William Whitelaw, chairman of the NBR from 1912 to 1923 and of the LNER from 1923 to 1938.

Stamp from the Nobel company in 1926, with a reputation for brilliant analysis and effective organisation. An American style was adopted, with Stamp as president of the executive, and four executive vice-presidents. Stamp was also appointed chairman in 1927. Concentration of decision-making at Euston increased, but he was a peripatetic president, travelling the system in a specially-fitted carriage (one Scottish executive referred to his visits as "sacking tours"). All but the most modest decisions had to be ratified, or taken, centrally. When the LMS arranged to "rescue" Hebridean steamer services by taking over the insolvent David MacBrayne company, jointly with Coast Lines, in 1928, it was Stamp who did the negotiating.

Inherited joint concerns were dealt with by a joint LMS/LNER committee: these were the joint stations at Aberdeen and Perth, Dentonholme Goods Station in Carlisle, the Dumbarton & Balloch and Dundee & Arbroath joint lines, the Grangemouth and Princes Dock branches; and the inherited Caledonian/North British Agreement of 1908. Competitive railway services did not disappear but were reduced even further. Both LMS and LNER ran trains between Edinburgh and Glasgow and between these cities and Aberdeen. Both ran services to London and the main English cities, the LMS using the Caledonian and Glasgow & South Western main lines; the LNER over the East Coast main line.

Signs of Change

Differences first noticed by the travelling public were a set of fare reductions, bringing the level of fares down from 75% to 50% above the pre-war rate (prices and incomes had doubled in the ten years from 1913). 'Foreign' locomotives and rolling stock began to appear, as the companies set out to rationalise their diverse inheritance of equipment. Caledonian engines came to the Highland, and Midland Railway engines became familiar on the former G&SW lines. New liveries were devised; at first LMS engines were painted 'Midland Red' before a more austere plain black was imposed. The LNER stuck to green for its passenger engines. St. Rollox, Kilmarnock, and Inverness works belonged to the LMS; the LNER had Cowlairs and Inverurie. All were kept in action, but after 1924 they built no more locomotives. In Glasgow the North British Locomotive Company continued to build new engines, mainly for export, but also Class A3, Pacifics, for the LNER and 'Royal Scot' 4-6-0s for the LMS. The old companies' works were seen as too small and too costly, and perhaps the presence of former chief mechanical engineers, working out their time as hardly more than works managers, was seen as an obstacle. A Scottish MP complained in 1923 that Scotland was losing out on orders for new carriages and wagons, "to the serious prejudice of trade and employment".

The road haulage industry, stimulated by the cheap sale of thousands of ex-military vehicles, was picking up more and more business that once would have had no alternative to the railway. The road hauliers knew the level of railway charges, which the companies were legally obliged to publish, and had plenty of margin to undercut them. Not only freight but passenger traffic was being lost. It became increasingly obvious that the 1921 Railways Act was not a blueprint for railway progress but a straitjacket that prevented the companies from competing on even terms with their new rivals. Sir Eric Geddes claimed from the sidelines that the railways just needed to be managed better, but he had misjudged the situation. Neither the LMS nor the LNER ever came near matching the 1913 level of earnings during their 24-year life, partly due to the slowness and inflexibility of the rate-fixing system, and much more to the new competitive environment, a failure which exerted a constant drag on their ability to innovate, cope with rising costs, and pay reasonable wages and a full range of dividends. At the time, though, the grouped railway companies still appeared huge and commercially dominant semi-monopolistic concerns, and received little political or public sympathy.

Industrial Unrest and the General Strike

For their employees, the new companies offered a much wider range of jobs for those willing to move, although particularly on the LMS, many senior posts were abolished as the old incumbent retired: there was only one company-wide head of each major department (in civil engineering it was Alexander Newlands, who had started out on the Highland Railway) and many competitors for vacancies. Wages became a source of friction as Britain's post-war economic boom changed to a mid-20s slump. In 1924 Whitelaw pointed out that while wages and salaries were 148% over their 1913 level, rates and charges were only between 50 and 60% above it. The ASLEF union had already mounted a strike in January of that year, in defence of enginemen's pay and conditions when the companies proposed a wage reduction in line with the (at the time) fall in the cost-of-living index, and the refusal of the National Union of Railwaymen to join them caused some hostility.

1925 was a dire year for the railways, with revenue falling steeply. Whitelaw called it the worst year ever, not knowing what 1926 would bring. In May that year the "Triple Alliance" of miners', railway and dock-workers' unions ceased work in the General Strike which began on 4 May. This was in support of the miners' dispute with the coal-owners. Most of the country's trade was immobilised. In the efforts to keep some trains running, the participation of volunteer workers was actively encouraged, under the protection of police and troops. Normal rules of train working were waived. A train driven by volunteers collided with wagons in the Calton Tunnel at Edinburgh on 13 May and three persons were killed. Resentments were running so high that the regular breakdown crew refused to assist. Industrial solidarity did not endure, however, and by 14 May railwaymen were returning to work, to find the companies taking a tough line, compelling the unions to accept that the action had been illegal and to commit themselves not to repeat it. James Calder told a strikers' deputation that they would be taken back "as and when there is work available for them". The miners' strike went on, with coal shortages forcing heavy cuts in train services into 1927.

Train Services in the Slump Years

Ever since the introduction of sleeping cars, requests for third class accommodation had been resisted by the railway companies. Both the LMS and LNER claimed there was no economic justification, but when in 1928 they yielded to public demand and began an "experimental" service from Edinburgh and Glasgow to London, it proved instantly successful and Inverness and Aberdeen also got third class sleepers that year. Occasional moments of flamboyance show that the era of movies and cinema news-reels had arrived. Even a little glamour could go a long way. On 27 April 1928, four days before the LNER introduced the non-stop 'Flying Scotsman' between London and Edinburgh, using Class A1 4-6-2s with corridor tenders for crew change, the LMS put on the "world's longest non-stop journey", running the 'Royal Scot' in separate Glasgow and Edinburgh portions from Euston. An ex-Midland 4-4-0 compound engine hauled the Edinburgh train, which arrived two minutes early; a new 'Royal Scot' 4-6-0 headed the Glasgow train, which arrived on time. It was a cheeky one-day wonder – the single train, dividing at Symington, resumed next day. At 8 hours 30 minutes for its 392-mile journey, the 'Flying Scotsman's' non-stop schedule was a 19th-century one, though improvement would come. Behind the window-dressing, most trains were using old rolling stock and running slowly behind engines of pre-Grouping design.

Freight still brought in much more revenue than passenger trains, and long-distance goods services were improved, with faster trains and more next-day deliveries for non-perishable items. The LNER published a timetable for the benefit of shippers, giving latest consignment times and scheduled arrival times for its best trains. Despite such efforts, customers continued to desert to the roads. In 1928 the LNER's revenue was £11,277,759, more than £3,500,000 short of the standard set by the 1921 Act, while the LMS, with revenue of £16,270,821, was £4,500,000 short.

The Railway Rates Tribunal permitted the companies to make a set of changes to goods rates in February 1928, following a reclassification of goods categories that had taken five years to complete. The urgency of the situation can be gauged by the example of cotton, both raw and manufactured, which had previously been carried almost entirely by rail, and was mostly now transported by road (76% in 1927, with only 24% by rail). The railways were desperate to have greater freedom to compete for and claw back traffic. A large-scale national road-building and improvement programme was going on, to the costs of which the railways, as large payers of local rates, were hapless contributors. In a remarkable gesture, the rail unions agreed in 1928 to accept a $2\frac{1}{2}\%$ cut in wages to help the companies in their financial plight. Shareholders found that the mighty LMS, famed as the world's largest joint-stock company, was unable to pay an Ordinary dividend that year.

More surprisingly, another company in difficulties at this time was the Scottish Motor Transport Co. (SMT) though its problem was lack of capital caused by over-rapid expansion, swallowing up a string of local bus operators across central Scotland. Railway companies had gained authorisation in 1927 to engage in road transport, and the LMS and LNER combined to recapitalise the SMT, each owning 25% of it. Their holdings produced a useful annual dividend through the 1930s but it remained an arm's length relationship and no attempt was made to align or integrate services.

As the slump intensified, the companies had to walk a precarious line to maintain services and revenue. Whitelaw told his shareholders in October 1929 that

"We have so much reduced fares that we have carried in the first 40 weeks of this year an increase of 10,000,000 passengers, and as a result we have received half a million pounds less as a reward for doing so." Yet an attempt to put fares up would have been refused as politically unacceptable. And in 1930 LNER passenger numbers fell back by 8,500,000, with freight tonnage 10,000,000 tons less than 1929. With the LMS in the same boat, Sir Josiah Stamp issued a message to his staff "of cheer and encouragement at what is probably the most difficult time in the history of railways and, indeed, in the economic history of the modern world … above all, we need to keep up our courage." Having restored the voluntary $2\frac{1}{2}\%$ pay cut in 1931, the companies succeeded in enforcing new reductions via the National Wages Board later in the same year. In 1932 a new and extensive traffic pooling system was agreed, to eliminate loss-inducing competition, saving train miles and staff costs. That year, LMS revenues were down £5 million (7.35%) on 1931, but its expenses were down by 7.79%, by dint of "modernisation", wage cuts, improvements in organisation, and withdrawals of unremunerative services. Staff cuts had helped: 15,931 had gone in 1931, half paid off, the others retired, resigned or died. Most losses were in the engineering shops.

The LMS closed around 20 Scottish passenger services in the 1930s, mostly village branches like those to Bankfoot, Edzell and Methven; the LNER rather fewer, including the Invergarry & Fort Augustus, Kincardine-Dunfermline, Leadburn-Dolphinton, and Gifford and Macmerry branches. Aberdeen's suburban trains to Dyce and Banchory were withdrawn from 5 April 1937, killed off by buses. Among the few total closures was the Solway Junction Railway in 1931 (the viaduct was demolished). On most lines little beyond basic maintenance was done, though one

At 1,531 feet above sea level, Wanlockhead was the highest station on a standard gauge railway in Britain until the LMS closed the branch in 1939. Ex-Caledonian No 228, here fitted with a spark arrester, was built in 1913 and withdrawn in 1962. The carriages came from another LMS outpost, the Garstang & Knott End Railway in Lancashire, closed in 1930. (John Alsop Collection)

welcome improvement was the LNER's installation of colour-light signalling on the smoke-filled City and District Underground line across central Glasgow in 1931. On the LMS especially, only new developments that embraced efficiency and economy were acceptable, like the new electrically-operated signal box at St. Enoch Station, which in 1933 replaced five lever-operated boxes.

Advances and Improvements

Much more was possible, in theory at least. In April 1931 the Committee on Railway Electrification, headed by the dynamic Scottish industrialist Lord Weir, reported to the Secretary of State for Transport, Tom Johnston (the Kirkintilloch-born MP who would later set up the North of Scotland Hydro-Electric Board), recommending a programme of electrification of Britain's main-line railways at an estimated cost of £261 million plus an £80 million investment by the new Central Electricity Generating Board. This was a vast sum, but the Committee pointed out that some £500 million had been spent on upgrading the road network since 1921, in a totally unplanned way. With bank rate at 2%, large loans could have been raised. The Government did not pursue it, and though his general manager Sir Ralph Wedgwood had been a member of Weir's committee, Whitelaw said the LNER could not afford the option of electrification. Nor was Stamp in favour: noting in 1930 that electrification of Glasgow suburban railways would cost £15 million, he said that such advances "were under constant review", company jargon for no action. Though a few diesel-powered shunting engines were acquired in the 1930s, the focus was firmly on steam power, both companies experimenting with high-pressure locomotives (to no avail). As a gesture to the past, the LMS agreed in 1932 to preserve the Highland Railway 'Jones Goods' No. 103, Britain's first 4-6-0 locomotive for home railways.

Improvements were made on some express services, primarily London-Edinburgh and London-Glasgow, with 20 minutes pared off the 'Royal Scot's' timing in May 1932, Euston to Glasgow, 7 hours 55 minutes, and the 'Flying Scotsman' (non-stop) now doing Kings Cross-Waverley in 7 hours 27 minutes in July of the same year, with specially-built trains. The LNER's 'Northern Belle' cruise train, introduced in 1933 as a £20 all-first class 2,000-mile seven-day excursion from London to the Highlands and the 'Scott country', in another specially-constructed set of carriages, was both criticised as a wasteful luxury and admired as a feat of marketing. It was re-run twice that year and its cruises continued until 1938 (it has been reinvented in the 21st century). In urban areas, peak demand could be very high, and somehow the companies managed to cope. In July 1933, during one of the 20th century's finest summers, slump or not, the LMS ran 900 special trains in the Glasgow Fair period, and the LNER put on 250. On one day that month the LNER carried 10,000 day trippers to and from Portobello, with twelve specials on top of the normal service. The trains were likened to "a huge bathing club." Taking advantage of the long daylight, evening excursion trips proved very popular. Large numbers of carriages were still kept for special use: mostly elderly stock of written-down value which could be deployed for events from curling matches to Highland Games and flower shows. In April 1938 26 LNER specials took 15,000 passengers to London to see Scotland beat England 1-0 at Wembley, and 45 LMS specials carried 28,000. It was a social necessity to have trains laid on in this way. Car ownership was still very limited and bus companies had few spare vehicles.

A Square Deal Wanted

Shareholders were alarmed by the slide in railway revenues and in 1932 the Scottish

Railway Stockholders Association merged with its English counterpart, also with the Railway Reform League and the LNER Stockholders Association, in the British Railway Stockholders' Union. In 1933 the two companies' revenues were less than half the standard set by the 1921 Act, and neither dared apply for an increase in rates and fares in case the resultant fall in traffic would make things even worse. LMS dividends were generally more regular and greater than those of the LNER, which failed on several occasions to pay anything to the holders of Ordinary shares. By 1934 it was being felt that the British economy had turned the corner and commercial life was picking up again. In July the LNER impressed schoolboys and many others by displaying its imposing new 2-8-2 'Mikado' express engine, *Cock o' the North*, at Waverley Station, the first of eight Class P2 locomotives specially designed to haul heavy trains, especially sleeper trains, on the Edinburgh-Aberdeen line. In 1934-35 there was much discussion about reorganising the railways of central Edinburgh, concentrating traffic either in a new two-level Princes Street Station or a rebuilt Waverley, with Princes Street becoming a bus terminal, but these remained only paper plans.

On 10 December 1937 the worst crash of the decade happened at Castlecary, on the former Edinburgh & Glasgow line. During a blizzard the 4.03 Edinburgh-Glasgow express ran into the rear of the 2 pm Dundee-Glasgow, causing the deaths of 35 people and injuring 67. A signalman's mistake was blamed. This was the country's most intensively-used main line and the LNER rather belatedly announced in August 1938 that the Hudd system of automatic train control would be installed on 250 engines working between Waverley and Queen Street. This had not been done by the time war broke out in September 1939, and the scheme was shelved.

Railway managers were chafing more and more against the obstructions still preventing them from competing on a level field with the road hauliers. They were still bound by the conditions set out in the 1921 Act, with some alleviation from 1933, when they were allowed to quote "exceptional rates" in a band between 5% and 40% below the standard maximum. But these needed approval from the Railway Rates Tribunal, and the railways were still forbidden to make special deals with individual customers. Every exceptional rate had to be entered in rate books at relevant stations, and these had to be open for public inspection, making it easy for the road contractors to undercut them. In 1937, permission was granted for a 5% rise

LNER Class P2 No. 2005 *Thane of Fife* entered traffic on 8 August 1936. It was based at Tay Bridge depot, Dundee, until its rebuilding as a 4-6-2 in 1942-43.

in goods and passenger rates. With ample evidence of the drain of custom, a 'Square Deal' campaign for the railways was launched in November 1938.

William Whitelaw resigned as LNER chairman that year, though he remained on the board of the Scottish Area. His successor, Sir Ronald Matthews, joined the other chairmen in putting their case to the Ministry of Transport and other bodies. Addressing the Glasgow Chamber of Commerce in February 1939, Stamp said the railways would have to take "drastic and revolutionary action" if their traffic continued to fall away: "in a subsidy-ridden Europe we are the only country that has not taken a penny out of the public pocket for the railway service." The campaign prodded the government into setting up a Transport Advisory Council which in May 1939 accepted that action was necessary. As with the Royal Commission in 1913, a state of war intervened, and despite renewed pleas from the companies and the Railway Shareholders' Protection Association, no action was taken during the ensuing period of government control.

As far as Scotland's rail users were concerned, the 1930s brought relatively little change. Apart from Anglo-Scottish services from the two main cities, speeds did not improve, though some amenities were added, with more trains incorporating restaurant or buffet cars. It was noted in 1936 that the most popular dish in the Northern Scottish section of the LNER was bacon and eggs; in Scotland 70% of passengers drank tea in preference to coffee, while in England the proportion was 50/50. Many stations, repainted in company colours in the 1920s, were in a dingy state by the end of the 30s, as were the majority of trains.

Neither company sought to increase its capital, though some advantage was taken of the government backing the interest payments on £30 million worth of loans to be made available to railway companies. Modernisation was most in evidence on the train running side. The LNER's efficient press office noted in January 1936 that in its current two-year programme it would build 207 engines, 1,154 passenger coaches, 11,046 wagons, 780 containers "of the latest type" (4-ton box containers) and would renew 466½ miles of track with 66,000 tons of British steel rails (the company's total route mileage amounted to 6,590). Mechanised coaling plants were installed at most of the busier locomotive depots, and cleaning equipment was installed at some depots. Nevertheless, in 1939, sixteen years after Grouping, the great majority of engines were still of pre-1923 design and construction. System-wide modernisation had not been accomplished. Wider economic circumstances, and the unintended shackles imposed by the 1921 Act, prevented the companies from doing more. How much more they would have done is an open question: dividends versus ploughed-back profits would have been a vexed issue. One is left with the feeling that just to keep these vast concerns running was sufficiently demanding for those in charge, without looking beyond the immediate horizon.

Motive Power and Rolling Stock, 1923-47

One provision of the 1921 Act had been for standardisation of equipment and the adoption of co-operative schemes of working. Of this there was virtually no sign. Locomotive development moved ahead most effectively on the LNER, where H.N. Gresley, its chief mechanical engineeer, enlarged and improved his range of fast 3-cylinder 'Pacific' engines, and from 1925 supplemented the North British 'Glen' 4-4-0s with fourteen K2 2-6-0 engines. The LMS continued to build outmoded and under-powered pre-Grouping types until 1927 when the first of its 'Royal Scot' class 4-6-0s was exhibited to the public at Edinburgh, Glasgow, Dundee and Aberdeen in November. New saloon-type cars were introduced for the 'Royal Scot' train, including a first class lounge car with 'boudoir-compartment'. Locomotive development in the 1930s showed perhaps the most extreme example of Gresley's practice of building relatively small classes of engine to operate on particular routes, with the imposing though problematic eight-strong P2 class introduced from 1936. The six Class K4 2-6-0s of 1937 were also built specially for the West Highland line. On the LMS, Stamp and the chief mechanical engineer W.A. Stanier, took the opposite view, with Stanier's Class 5 'general utility' engine, introduced in 1935, working passenger and goods trains everywhere between Wick and Bournemouth. After Gresley, the LNER would also adopt this policy, with Edward Thompson's B1 4-6-0 class of 1942.

Gresley was also innovative in carriage design, saving train weight by building articulated carriages, two bodies mounted on three bogies. In the 1930s, wood was still a prime component in carrriage bodies, though with steel frames, but all-steel carriages were being built by the end of the decade, using assembly line techniques and pre-formed parts that greatly reduced building time. Both companies still ran gas- and even oil-lit carriages in 1930, though by 1939 oil was phased out and gas was rare.

The oldest engines, and those belonging to very small classes, were being scrapped, and by 1935 the LMS was operating with 24% fewer locomotives than in 1923. At the amalgamation it had 393 locomotive types; by 1938 the number was down to 220. Over 360 G&SWR engines were scrapped between 1923 and 1939, with only eleven surviving into the 1940s, compared with 54 Highland and 60 GNSR. In 1940 the bulk of Scottish locomotive stock was almost 750 Caledonian and 680 NBR engines, working branches, secondary services and almost all freight trains.

George Robertson, stationmaster at Waverley between 1927 and May 1940, in full top-hat rig, has a word with the driver of Class A4 No 4482, *Golden Eagle*, on the 'Flying Scotsman', in 1938. (Arjan den Boer/Creative Commons)

World War II and Nationalisation

State Control Again

Through 1939 it was increasingly clear that war was coming, and the railway companies made detailed provision. In July intensive planning for evacuation was going on in the Scottish areas. Glasgow, Edinburgh, Clydebank and Dundee, also the communities adjoining the Forth Bridge, were listed for evacuation of children. When the order "Evacuate forthwith" was given on 31 August, the plans clicked into action. In three days, 123,639 evacuees were moved from Glasgow and Clydebank, and in all around 176,000 children were moved to a wide range of places like Buchlyvie, Comrie, Turriff and Wigtown, with stations from which buses, cars or carts could take them to nearby places. It was another tribute to communal organising capacity and to railway efficiency, though it turned out to have been a premature precaution. In the first "phoney war" phase the anticipated aerial attacks did not happen, and by Christmas three quarters of the evacuees had been brought back to their homes.

Resumption of total war, after a twenty year gap, meant that many railway workers at all levels had already experienced war conditions. They knew what to do and got on with it. There had already been discussions with the government about how the railways would be managed and financed if war broke out: the railway boards remembered the enforced post-war settlement of 1921 and did not want a repetition. Once again the government was taking control, keeping all the receipts and paying back fixed amounts. The companies suggested hopefully that the "standard revenue" of 1921 should be the basis, but they had never earned as much as that, and instead, payments were to be based on their averaged actual revenues of the years 1935-37, amounting to £40 million. If the total revenue in a war year should exceed that, the extra up to £43,500,000 would be shared, with 34% going to the LMS and 23% to the LNE. Any surplus beyond that, up to £56 million, would go half to the government and half to the companies. Anything above £56 million would be taken wholly by the government. The companies did not regard this as particularly equitable, but with hostile voices saying their share was too big, it was not a time to seem greedy and unpatriotic, and they accepted what was on offer. This time government traffic was not carried free but at anything down to a third less than the standard rates. In December 1940 the terms were revised: the

Children evacuated from Glasgow arrive at Dunning Station, September 1939

companies were to share £43 million a year and everything over that went to the government. Damage from enemy attack was provided for, up to a point: £10 million from the 'control account' could be paid in any one year, with any extra paid by the companies, subject to "any general compensation which the government may ultimately pay" after the end of hostilities. With the inevitable rise in traffic created by war production, the government earned more from the railways than the companies themselves did – £45,700,000 in 1942 and £62 million in 1943, the peak year of the war for railway earnings.

The Wartime Railway

Working timetables for wartime conditions had been prepared before war was declared, and the companies, and the nation, settled into wartime mode. Once again the Highlands and Islands were declared a Protected Area, from 27 February 1940, with passes required for entry to the region. The nature of warfare had changed and the need for a 'blackout' against air attack made many operations, especially shunting, more difficult and dangerous, and the number of accidents increased. The blackout, together with rationing of food and many other commodities, including cigarettes, encouraged pilfering: more than a million towels were stolen from carriage lavatories in 1941-42. Huge numbers of light bulbs were also removed, despite being the wrong voltage for domestic use. Troop movements were constant, including the return of the 24-hour 'Misery' between Euston and Thurso, and by January 1940 volunteer canteens were providing refeshments for servicemen and women on the move at all transfer stations between Dingwall and Dumfries.

Following the sudden Clydeside blitz of May 1941, an evacuation scheme was reintroduced in Greenock, Dumbarton and Port Glasgow, but though sporadic air raids continued at various locations, primarily east coast towns and Edinburgh, and an attempt on the Lochaber aluminium plant was made in 1941, there was no further intensive bombing, and most children soon returned home. The great East Coast bridges, defended by anti-aircraft batteries, survived the attentions of the *Luftwaffe*. Josiah Stamp (a baron since 1938) was killed when his house in Kent was hit by a bomb on the night of 16 April 1941. His place as LMS chairman was taken by Sir Thomas (later Lord) Royden, more remote as a public figure but who maintained Stamp's general line of management, until 1946.

Perhaps the most intensively-used lines were those of the former Caledonian and Glasgow & South Western to Greenock. On 6 October 1939 a special train brought £6 million worth of gold bullion, to be shipped to Canada for safe keeping, and very many more workaday shipments went both outwards and inwards. From America's entry into the war in 1941, traffic increased enormously. Between May 1942 and December 1944, 339 troopships docked at Greenock, disembarking 1,319,089 servicemen, the vast majority of whom were carried onwards by train. The transatlantic influx of war materials and soldiers placed demands on the railway service far beyond what was anticipated when the war payment terms were agreed. New harbours were constructed to supplement and if necessary replace the older Clyde ports. In the south west, a branch line of $5\frac{1}{2}$ miles and a large railway installation were laid to serve the military port of Cairnryan, north of Stranraer, begun on 20 January 1941 and operational by 20 July 1942. Another branch of $2\frac{1}{2}$ miles was laid from the West Highland line to Faslane on the Firth of Clyde in 1941. Craigendoran was also taken over as an emergency port in October 1940. In many places crossing loops were laid or extended to speed up trains. Little-used cross-country lines like Carstairs-Dolphinton-Leadburn, long closed to passengers, saw new traffic as trains were re-routed to avoid main-line congestion. Few lines

Former NBR 'Atlantic' No. 904, *Holyrood*, now LNER No. 9904, at Waverley in the 1930s.
(Stenlake Collection)

were closed, other than the branch from Wick to Lybster, in 1944. From March 1941 an Inter-Railway Freight Rolling Stock Control system was operated, to ensure that wagons, especially coal wagons, and vans were distributed in accordance with traffic needs.

Although railway work was a protected occupation, by 1943 15% of the LNER's male staff were in the armed forces, and one in six of its 33,000 employees was female. At Perth, the women porters got the porters' mess-room and space was found for male porters in an annex to the gents' toilets. As in World War I, with the cost of living rising, wage increments were paid, notionally on a temporary basis, though no-one could prophesy conditions when peace eventually returned.

A New Policy

The generation born in the early 1920s, coming of age around 1944, had witnessed the aftermath of World War I, industrial strife, the Great Depression, and World War II. Most of them had few reasons to feel that the old order of things had been satisfactory. As the prospect of eventual victory became more assured, a resolve that the future should be different became more clearly defined, and a political programme was widely debated, which included state ownership of the basic industries: coal mining, iron and steel, electricity and gas, long-distance road transport, air transport, and the railways. Railway nationalisation was a far older issue than the others, going back to Gladstone's ideas a hundred years earlier, and occasionally revived when charges and facilities became an issue – most recently in 1918-20. Railway directors were fully aware of this and joined in the debate about their companies' future. They too wanted a new dispensation that gave greater commercial freedom. Even Whitelaw, always the most vocal defender of shareholders' interests, backed an LNER proposal that the government should take ownership of the rail network and let the companies operate the trains – an intriguing presaging of what would happen in 2002. From 1942 onwards, the companies ran publicity campaigns to emphasise their contribution to the nation and highlight the problems that state ownership would bring – not an easy task since they were currently functioning very effectively as a single state-controlled organisation. Citing their own record in the 1930s of maintaining services, making technical improvements, and social responsibility in holding rates and fares steady, they made it clear that they were willing and able to meet the post-war challenges. There was certainly an element of truth in that, even if fares had been held steady by the fear that increases would be self-defeating. Within the companies a real feeling existed that the railways were a public service and not merely commercial concerns. Knowing too that public opinion was against them, they had to be careful not to seem to be trying to turn the clock back to the pre-war era, and the LNER formed a Post-War Development Committee which proposed a range of new plans: the reconstruction of Waverley, Queen Street and Dundee (Tay Bridge) Stations, electrification of the line through Queen Street (Low Level) and a new marshalling yard at Edinburgh.

By the end of the war, Scottish railways, relatively unscathed by enemy action, were in a run-down rather than damaged state. Maintenance had been on a priority basis, and rolling stock, much of it dating back to pre-1923, was dilapidated and ingrained with dirt and soot. With peace restored, more people wanted to travel, and did not relish the condition of their trains, while the previous standard reply to all complaints, "Don't you know there's a war on?" would no longer do. In an almost-bankrupt Great Britain, faced with huge reconstruction costs and international debt, the railway companies found it difficult to impress the travelling public, though they tried hard to restore service levels and to demonstrate plans for an effective future. That of course might include cutting costs wherever possible, and West Perthshire saw protests in October 1945 against the LMS's intention to close the line between Crieff and Balquhidder. A Strathearn Railway Committee was set up, staving off execution to 1951.

The Grouping had been a compromise between private enterprise and state control, and failed because the model did not correspond to actual conditions: the companies could neither satisfy their shareholders nor modernise to the degree that was technically possible and socially desirable. Now a new dispensation was to be tried.

Nationalisation: the Creation of Scottish Region

In the 1945 general election, 37 of Scotland's 71 seats were won by Labour, three by Independent Labour, and one by the Communist Party. With an overwhelming Parliamentary majority, the new Labour Government embarked on its nationalisation programme. For two years, the railway companies lived on borrowed time, continuing to do all the things that would have been expected of companies with a future. New locomotive types were introduced, including Britain's first main-line express diesel-electric engines, working successfully on LMS main lines. The LNER built 60 new express 'Pacifics'. But the buffers were coming into sight. A new Transport Act was passed in August 1947, providing for state ownership not just of the railway system but of most transport services except for those operating on a local basis (25 miles radius or less), under the control of a British Transport Commission.

The Chancellor of the Exchequer, Hugh Dalton, offended many railway people in describing the railways as "a very poor bag of physical assets" and a "disgrace to the nation", so shortly after they had made a vital, sustained and exhausting contribution to the nation's war effort. Sir Ronald Matthews of the LNER condemned the terms of Nationalisation as such as "would bring a blush of shame to the leathery cheeks of a Barbary pirate", but most economic historians agree that they were not unreasonable. Based on the Stock Exchange valuation of railway shares, railway shareholders were issued with £907.8 million of 3% British Transport Commission stocks, with annual 3% interest guaranteed by the government. LMS Ordinary shareholders got £29 10s of BTC 3% shares for every £100; LNER shareholders got £7 6s. Interest payments, at £27.2 million a year, were to prove a heavy burden on the new BTC.

At the last ordinary general meeting of LNER shareholders, in March 1948, the proposal to reward the directors with the sum of £63,000 was lost on a show of hands; instead the last dividend on 5% Preference Ordinary shares was raised from 18s 2d% to 19s 2d%.

One effect of Nationalisation was to finally confirm the position of the railways as a general national utility, ending their ambivalent relationship with the state as privately-owned corporations working under government-imposed conditions and limits. Ironically this happened just as the switch in emphasis from railway to road was about to become definitive. A vital ambiguity still remained, however, which the Act of 1947 failed to address. Was the new British Railways intended to maintain and provide a nationwide service, or was it intended to operate profitably on behalf of the nation? The railways' shrinking role in ground transport had been obvious for two decades, while they still bore the burden of being 'common carrier' to the nation. The fact that they were still profitable, taken as a whole, obscured this issue.

The British Transport Commission was set up from 1 January 1948, headed by Sir Cyril Hurcomb, a former Permanent Secretary to the Ministry of Transport, with a set of executive bodies to manage specific sections of the industry: a Railway

LNER class O6 locomotive No. 7655 with a breakdown train near Kelso, 10 January 1946. The locomotive was one of 60 built by the LNER to LMS designs during the war and was considered LMS stock. It had a brief history in the LNER before it was handed over to the LMS later in October 1947.(Stenlake Collection)

Executive, a Docks and Waterways Executive, a Road Transport Executive and a London Transport Executive. A Hotels Executive was also added to take over railway-managed hotels, of which fifteen were in Scotland. From the Scottish point of view, the most important aspect of the 1947 Act was that the new system was to be divided into six regions, five in England and Wales, and a Scottish Region combining the Scottish sections of the LMS and LNER. This had been strongly argued for both by Scottish MPs and by Scottish peers in the House of Lords. For the first time, albeit as a division of an organisation whose central HQ was in London, the Scottish railways were to be administered as a single entity. The new Region had 3,730 route miles and 3,957 miles of sidings, and employed 31,640 men and 3,650 women.

Regional autonomy was not on the agenda: the British Transport Commission and Railway Executive were determined to operate British Railways as one vast integrated enterprise, exercising central control on all aspects, and seeing regional managements as agents to implement national policy. Friction arose very soon between Commission and Executive over which was to formulate policy, and how instructions should be passed to the regions. As the English regions were based very much on the former companies' territories, the BTC feared they would tend to revert to the old pattern. In Scotland this was less of a problem as the new region had the task of combining ex-LMS and ex-LNER staff and systems into one. Chief regional officer for Scotland was T.F. Cameron, LNER Scottish general manager since 1946, at an annual salary of £3,750 (his London Midland Region colleague earned £7,500), and Scottish interests were represented on the BTC by a part-time board member, Sir Ian Bolton, a Glasgow accountant, who saw his role more in terms of representing the commission to Scotland. A pale shade of blue, faintly reminiscent of the Caledonian's blue, was assigned as the Scottish Region's colour, as a background to nameboards and other station signs.

The BTC and Scottish Region

The new regional management had an early test with the disastrous floods of August 1948, when torrential rain in the eastern Borders caused massive damage to railway lines and much else. Reaction was prompt and effective. The Edinburgh-Berwick main line was closed for eleven weeks while temporary bridges were speedily built and southbound trains diverted down the Waverley Route as far as St. Boswells, then along the former North British and North Eastern lines via Kelso to Tweedmouth. Some dauntless drivers succeeded in taking the 'Flying Scotsman' non-stop along this emergency route. The almost-parallel line between St. Boswells and Reston Junction was breached west of Earlston, and though the track was restored, the passenger service between St. Boswells and Duns was not. The Jedburgh branch, also flooded, was reinstated for goods traffic only.

Cameron and his team were closely involved with the Glasgow and District Transport Committee, chaired by Sir Robert Inglis, another former general manager of the LNER Scottish Division, which sat between 1949 and 1951 and produced a report which recommended the phasing out of the city's trams and electrification of the suburban railway network. It was an ambitious proposal which, though it did not attract the backing of the British Transport Commission, remained an obvious and desirable solution to the run-down and obsolescent condition of Glasgow's railways.

The experiment of creating a unified pan-British transport system came to an end with the return of a Conservative government in 1951, pledged to restore road haulage to private enterprise. A new Transport Act in 1953 provided for this and also abolished the Railway Executive, leaving the truncated BTC to run the railways with no intermediate tier of management between it and the regions, and with a brief – which the BTC hardly pursued – to devolve more authority to the regions. A new chairman, General Sir Brian Robertson, took over from Hurcomb in September 1953. From 1 January 1955, along with the other regions, the Scottish Region was provided with an advisory area board, intended to extend its links with business and commerce. Board chairman was Sir Ian Bolton and members included businessmen like Lord Bilsland (as Sir Steven Bilsland, a former member of the LMS Scottish committee). T.F. Cameron's title was altered from chief officer to general manager, but his executive authority was still limited. In 1956 he was allowed to agree expenditure of up to £50,000 (£100,000 from 1959) and make appointments up to the level of departmental head without reference to London. Robertson was as reluctant as Hurcomb to cede powers to the regions, and set up a somewhat army-style 'general staff' at the London headquarters, giving direct instructions to the regional functional heads.

The Scottish Region was geographically the largest of the BTC regions but not the biggest revenue earner, though the BTC did not publish separate accounts for the regions. Cameron retired in 1955 and was briefly succeeded by A.E.H. Brown, who died soon after taking office, and then by James Ness, whose career had begun with the North British in 1919 and who had held senior positions in the BTC headquarters staff. Cameron had done an excellent job in welding his two divisions of the former companies (still harbouring many memories of their predecessors) into a single entity, helped perhaps by the Scottish sense of identity; but to run a mix of local and suburban services in the densely-populated central belt and long-distance services across wide tracts of thinly-populated territory in the south west, Southern Uplands and the Highlands was a challenge. Passengers and freight customers were increasingly using the private car, the bus or coach, and the heavy lorry. Traffic innovations centred, as in the past, on Anglo-Scottish services, though now with popular rather than prestige trains. Cheap overnight 'Starlight Specials' introduced in 1953 between Glasgow (St. Enoch) and London (St. Pancras) and Edinburgh (Waverley) and London (Marylebone) succeeded in clawing back much business from the overnight coach services. A new non-stop Edinburgh-London express, the 'Elizabethan', was introduced in the Coronation year of 1953, taking 6 hours 45 minutes, with no supplementary fare. Internal services were run to much the same pattern, and with the same motive power and rolling stock, as pre-1948. By 1955 it was the worst-performing region in financial terms, and efforts had been made to pare away the most obviously unprofitable services. Lines like Inveramsay-Macduff (closed to passengers in 1951), Dundee's two lines to Strathmore (1955), and the Border Counties line from Hexham to Riccarton Junction (1956) were left only with a skeletal goods service. From Alford to Whithorn, 35 passenger services were withdrawn in Scotland between 1948 and 1953, seventeen of them in 1951.

One of the provisions of the 1947 Act had been the setting up of Transport Users' Consultative Committees, to consider the impact of transport service closures on users. The Scottish TUCC was set up in July 1949, with eighteen members, drawn from agriculture, commerce, industry, shipping, labour and local authorities, as well as nominees of the Ministry of Transport and the BTC. Its terms of reference were fairly narrow, centred on how much "hardship" a closure would entail, and it could do no more in opposing than pass a suggestion for delay or modification to the Minister of Transport. Even such opposition was rare, not least because the railway witnesses could present 'facts' whereas much of the opposers' evidence boiled down to feeling. At this time, when a general head of steam against railway closures had not yet built up, lay TUCC members might well defer to the certainties of the

Killin Station in the late 1950s with camping coach, looking east towards Ben Lawers. The line continues to Loch Tay Station, disused since September 1939, but the branch locomotive shed remained there. (Stenlake Collection)

professionals. Still, by 1950 the closure of under-used branches was becoming an issue. Lord Bilsland deplored the BTC's "defeatism" in pressing regions to shut down branch passenger services without prior attempts to improve traffic, and with no provision of alternative arrangements, but closures went ahead.

The *Princess Victoria* Disaster

Scottish Region was responsible for the operation of the steamer services inherited from the former companies. Investment here was essential as the steamer fleet was mostly elderly and depleted. Tragedy struck the Stranraer-Larne route when on 31 January 1953 the relatively new MV *Princess Victoria*, one of the first drive-on car ferry ships, foundered in the North Channel during a ferocious storm, with the loss of 133 lives. Five new general purpose vessels were launched for Firth of Clyde services in 1953, and a new *Maid of the Loch* for Loch Lomond. The new ships prompted a surge in usage: on Glasgow Fair Monday, 19 July 1954, they carried 48,000 people, twice the 1953 number.

The Modernisation Plan

British Railways was very much a steam-powered system and in the early 1950s was developing a set of standard steam locomotives which might be expected to have an operational life of twenty-five years or more. Up to 1960 almost 1,000 were built, of which 220 were allocated to Scottish depots for varying periods. Most engines now dated from the Grouping era, with many of the war-production 'Austerity' 2-8-0 freight engines and all 25 of the 2-10-0 types at work on freight services in central

Scotland (the great majority of these very effective engines were built in Glasgow), but around 130 Caledonian, almost 230 North British, and two Great North of Scotland veterans were still at work in 1960: a third of the Region's locomotive stock. In January 1950 the first of BR's ten 'Clan' Class Pacifics, *Clan Buchanan*, was displayed at Glasgow Central. They never operated on the former Highland line, as had apparently been intended; though *Clan Cameron* took a special train on the West Highland to Fort William in 1956, arranged by British Railways Board member Donald Cameron of Lochiel in connection with a clan celebration.

Greater government priorities meant relatively low investment in railways (and roads) from 1948 to 1954. Around £7 million was spent on new works in Scottish Region, the main project being the modernisation of Cadder marshalling yard at Bishopbriggs. By 1954 the railway scene was looking distinctly old-fashioned, still using much in the way of pre-war equipment and methods. Little had changed since the 1930s or even the 1920s, with many stations and signal boxes still lit by gas or oil lamps. Staff morale was low and it was difficult to retain workers in the heavy or dirtier jobs, like firing and cleaning. Cars were now in mass production and motorways were being actively planned. The British Transport Commission had to confront the issue, and in 1955 its Railway Modernisation Plan was published, setting out a strategy to be implemented within five years and completed within fifteen. It was intended to be a vision of the modern railway's place in national life as a major element in freight and passenger transport, and, of course, financially self-supporting. An investment of £1,240 million was anticipated, of which half was needed to bring the network up to the standards required by a modern railway. A central element was the gradual elimination of steam power. Electrification was seen as the ultimate goal, with diesel power as an interim stage. Some electrification schemes were proposed, including that of the Glasgow suburban network, and a new freight traffic pattern was set out, with closure of many small goods yards and

Kelso Station in the early 1960s with both diesel and steam trains. (Stenlake Collection)

the provision of large new marshalling yards. In Scotland these would be at Edinburgh, Mossend, Thornton, Perth and Alloa. A modern marshalling yard at Edinburgh had been projected since 1923. The Modernisation Plan was widely welcomed, quickly approved by Sir Anthony Eden's Conservative government, and implementation went ahead.

Change soon became visible as diesel traction spread, and long lines of redundant steam locomotives stood dead on sidings. Another link to the past vanished when the last of Scotland's railway horses were retired from the end of May 1955. New engines and wagons fitted with automatic brakes made new express goods services possible: from August 1955 the 'Hielan' Piper' ran nightly between Paisley, Glasgow, Aberdeen and Inverness, and was followed in 1956 by the 'Killie' between Aberdeen, Perth, Stirling, Glasgow, Irvine and Kilmarnock. By 1958 the region was running 80 Class C 'fitted' freight trains daily, more than any other. This initiative was followed up by a next-day 'assured arrival' service for smaller items from Glasgow and Edinburgh to Dundee, Aberdeen, Elgin and Inverness, from April 1959. In 1959 the 'Condor' (container door-to-door) express began running from Gushetfaulds freight depot to Hendon in London, claimed as the fastest long-distance goods train in Europe. These initiatives were helped by the railways' new ability, under the 1953 Act, to exercise what James Ness described as "relative charging freedom" negotiating carriage deals with customers. Nothing happened too fast: charges still had to be approved by the Transport Tribunal (successor from 1948 of the Railway Rates Tribunal) and it was not until 1957 that the railways finally got free of the 'common carrier' and other obligations of the Cardwell Act of 1854. Another successful introduction was the drive-on car-sleeper service introduced between London and Perth in 1955; three years later there were five Anglo-Scottish car-sleepers. Diesel railcars were tried out in 1956 on the Crieff and Galashiels lines, and a battery-powered railcar on the Deeside line in 1958. The new marshalling yard at Thornton opened in January 1956. Electrification of the line from Helensburgh, through Queen Street (Low Level) and on to Airdrie was put in hand.

The Reappraisal

So much appeared positive, yet during the second half of the decade railway usage was slumping and financial losses, exacerbated by the costs of the modernisation programme, growing hugely. The welcome given to the Modernisation Plan in 1955 soon turned into harsh criticism. While it had achieved a great deal, its operational strategy lay in ruins. This was not wholly the fault of its authors, who had no idea that their fifteen-year timetable would coincide with the inexorable shrinkage of heavy industry. Coal, iron and steel, shipbuilding – in every industrial district the smokestacks were toppling and the cranes being dismantled. But their hastily-confected plan had taken scant account of what had already been clear: the changed transport requirements of a society owning and using cars on a hugely-increasing basis. Replacing old trains with new on services for which demand was in steady decline could at best only briefly stem the fall in traffic. They also showed over-haste in what became a dash for complete dieselisation. Too many new types were ordered without proper trials and were found to have problems only after being put into line service. Worst example was Scottish Region's Type 21, of which 58 were built between 1958 and 1960 by the North British Locomotive Company in Glasgow. Hopelessly prone to breakdown, spurned by other regions, they lived out brief and ineffectual lives based at Eastfield Depot. The builders went into liquidation in 1962. The railways' share of passenger traffic, 21.4% in 1951-53, was down to 14.3% in 1960-62 and their freight share fell from 45.3% to 29.2%.

Service cuts would of course have generated national protest – it would need a strong new vision of what the railways were about before such a policy could be forced through, and that was not achievable in the 1950s. In 1958 BTC Chairman Robertson was still insisting that merchandise traffic in less than wagon-load consigments could be retained by "proper charging and good service". On a visit to Scotland in October 1959, he announced that "The Commission are adopting a very bold forward policy in Scotland. Undeterred by the fact that the setbacks in the heavy industries … are gravely affecting our traffic receipts, we are intensifying our efforts to modernise this part of our system, and we are showing faith in Scotland's economic future."

What of the railway staff, whose need for a boost in morale was specifically noted in the Modernisation Plan? While so much was being invested in modern equipment, railway wages were slipping down the industrial scale. A judicial inquiry into railway pay in 1954 established the principle that parity with private industry should be maintained, and this was reaffirmed in March 1960 by the joint BTC and union sponsored inquiry into railway pay headed by C.W. Guillebaud. But successive governments would press British Railways to link pay rises to productivity. To the unions productivity meant job losses, fewer members, and less influence, as well as the prospect of higher pay and possibly better conditions for retained workers, which made it difficult for both sides to keep up a constructive dialogue. The Modernisation Plan's failure to generate surpluses left the management squeezed between the need to pay competitive wages and pressure from government to hold down costs, and railway pay levels continued to slip back by comparison with other industries.

Freight at Thurso Station, July 1969. (Stenlake Collection)

A Decade of Radical Change – the 1960s

Enter Dr Beeching

Sir Brian Robertson said of the Glasgow electrification, "there will be no better rolling stock on any suburban service in the Kingdom. It has, as you know, been built in Scotland" (the car bodies were built at Linwood). Phase 1 was completed in November 1960 and the Class 303 'Blue Trains' were launched with much ado. Soon, however, it became clear that there was something wrong. Explosions and fires indicated serious problems with the transformers, and on 30 December the Region withdrew the new trains until matters could be investigated and rectified. An emergency steam-powered service was hastily restored – no easy task as much of the necessary infrastructure for steam power had already been cleared away. Staff rallied valiantly to achieve it, but the travelling public was understandably unimpressed. The electric trains returned after nine months, from 1 October 1961.

The summer of 1962 saw the end of non-stop trains between Waverley and Kings Cross. The new 3300hp 'Deltic' locomotives made a stop at Newcastle to change crews (the journey took six hours, matching the pre-war 'Coronation' but with three trains each way daily). Gresley's A4 'Pacifics', transferred to the Edinburgh and Glasgow to Aberdeen route, matched diesel timings.

While maintaining business as usual, railway managers at all levels could not fail to realise that things had gone badly wrong. Even as modernisation went ahead, the system was heavily losing revenue both in its core freight traffic and its still nationwide passenger services. In 1959 a Conservative government was re-elected and Ernest Marples was appointed Minister of Transport. A House of Commons Select Committee on the Nationalised Industries noted in July 1960 that the BTC was caught in a conflict between social and economic viability in its provision of services. Marples appointed an advisory committee, headed by the industrialist Sir Ivan Stedeford, to look at the structure, finance and working of the BTC. Stedeford's report criticised the BTC as non-commercial in outlook, obscure in organisation, and unclear in its objectives, particularly as far as its "social" mission was concerned. The report was not made public. One committee member in particular impressed Marples: Dr Richard Beeching, seconded from Imperial Chemical Industries. Robertson retired in 1961 and Beeching was appointed BTC chairman, with a

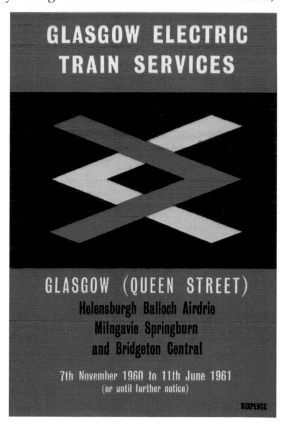

Timetable for the new electric train services with their double arrow logo. (Hutton Collection)

87

A Park Royal type railbus on a Stirling-Dollar service, around 1960. The Devon Valley line passenger service was withdrawn in 1964. (North British Railway Study Group)

brief to review the entire range of railway operations and recommend a strategy for a profitable system.

Rapid action followed. In August 1962 a traffic survey was conducted in Scotland and revealed that 2,000 of the 2,750 daily services ran at a loss. Cuts to save £450,000 a year were proposed, but deferred by union protests. A new Transport Act in 1962 abolished the British Transport Commission and set up the British Railways Board in its place, with a set of regional boards, including Scotland, and this came into operation on 1 January 1963 (the well-known BR two-way arrows logo was introduced in 1965). Engineering works were hived off into a separate management unit. Beeching, chairman of the new British Railways Board, and his team were already hard at work analysing the traffic patterns and revenues of the system, and drawing conclusions. Under the title *The Reshaping of British Railways,* his findings were passed to the Ministry of Transport and published in March 1963. They caused a tremendous storm and a great deal of dismay. Unprofitable services, lines and stations were to be cut, reducing the network by more than a third.

In Scotland, 51 passenger train services were up for withdrawal, with more than 1,000 miles of route. Every line from Aberdeen except those to the south and to Inverness, every line north of Inverness, the lines from Ayr and Dumfries to Stranraer, the Waverley Route, Dunblane-Crianlarich, the Fife Coast, and many branches were slated for closure. Local authorities, other organisations, and thousands of individuals combined to fight the proposed closures. Reaction in the north was particularly strong, organised under the (already anachronistic) 'MacPuff' banner, and succeeded in retaining the Wick/Thurso and Kyle lines. In 1963 Scotland had 32 Tory and 38 Labour MPs, and one Liberal, with a general election looming. Eight Tories would lose their seats in 1964, though railway closures were only one issue, and the incoming Labour government would maintain the closure policy for four years. Despite intense opposition, the 'Port Road' to Stranraer was closed in 1965, and the Waverley Route followed in 1969. A venture to purchase that line and run it as a private concern failed to raise sufficient capital. Dr Beeching returned to ICI in 1964, and by 1970 his "surgery" had been accomplished. Scotland's 3,138 route miles in 1963 were reduced to 1,954; 671 passenger stations were cut to 283, and 124 freight points survived out of 963. Staff numbers had been more than halved, from 47,063 to 22,462.

After the Cuts

Scottish Region had no option but to act on decisions made in London, but its chiefs appear to have considered the closure policy largely desirable – running public services that the public isn't using is not much fun, even for an inwards-looking management, focused on systems and with an ingrained culture of deference to upper levels of the organisation. Closures combined with falling traffic to make parts of the still unfinished Modernisation Plan redundant before completion. By the end of 1967 there were no steam locomotives working in Scotland, but Perth's huge marshalling yard lay largely unused; Thornton's worked at half-capacity, and even Millerhill, opened in 1963, though it made freight working in the Edinburgh area more efficient, was much larger than now seemed necessary. Passenger numbers actually went up during the closure years, from 65.8 million in 1966 to 68.5 million in 1969, with receipts rising from £14.47 million to £16.7 million. Positive changes went ahead also: in 1962 coal traffic flow was improved by the Craiglockhart Spur linking the line from Carstairs to the South Suburban in Edinburgh and giving access to the Millerhill yard. The South Clyde electric trains, introduced in August 1962, carried 150,000 people in their first week, three times the previous loading. In January 1965 electrification to Wemyss Bay and Gourock was announced; and Britain's first regular merry-go-round coal trains began between Monktonhall Colliery and the new Cockenzie Power Station in 1966. Beeching had identified container freight as a profit centre, and Freightliner terminals opened in Aberdeen and Edinburgh in 1968. Elimination of stations on surviving lines enabled faster timings, though the speedings-up hailed with each new timetable were of no value to those whose stations were closed.

The entrance to Queen Street Station shortly before the closure of Glasgow's tram system in 1962. Route 1 ran from Knightswood or Kelvinside to Airdrie. (Author's Collection)

Among other issues was the on-going dialogue with the unions, centred on productivity. New technology and new work methods all ended up in reduction of staff numbers, the most obvious examples being no need for a fireman in a locomotive without a fire and designed to be driven by one man; or for a guard and brake van on a freight train fitted with continuous automatic brakes. Weapons of industrial dispute, working to rule, strikes, go-slows, were deployed as the rail unions fought first for jobs to be retained, then for pay levels to rise in line with the responsibility of one-man engine operation, and of signalmen who had to master electronic systems covering dozens of miles. Productivity – more revenue from fewer staff, was what the management sought, while the unions argued that a share of the productivity savings should go to the workforce. Eventually the old railway job descriptions gave way to a new set of job titles: railman, senior railman, leading railman, chargeman, with pay differentials based partly on length of service and partly on responsibility. Much of the productivity savings were absorbed by higher costs, not only in wages and salaries but also of equipment.

British Railways Board

PUBLIC NOTICE

Transport Act. 1962

WITHDRAWAL OF RAILWAY PASSENGER SERVICES

The Minister of Transport having given her approval under powers conferred by the Transport Act. 1962, the Scottish Region of British Railways announce that all passenger train services between GLASGOW BUCHAN-AN STREET and SIGHTHILL EAST JUNCTION will be discontinued and

GLASGOW (BUCHANAN STREET)
Passenger Station

will be closed on and from

MONDAY 7th NOVEMBER, 1966

From this date passenger services and facilities meantime provided at Glasgow Buchanan Street Passenger Station will be available at Glasgow Queen Street Passenger Station.

An alternative rail service for Cumbernauld travellers will be available via Springburn and the Glasgow North Electric services. Full details of this and other services to be run from Glasgow Queen Street Passenger Station are contained in a pamphlet which can be obtained at stations towards the end of October.

Closure of Buchanan Street Station is announced for 7 November 1966. (British Railways)

An era of drastic change brought changes to the management organisation. James Ness left in 1963 to join BR's HQ team in London, and W.G. Thorpe took over as general manager, becoming also chairman of the area board in 1964. Under Thorpe a simplified two-tier management unique to the Scottish Region was adopted. District offices were closed, and three Traffic divisions, Glasgow & South West, Edinburgh (and the east up to Elgin), and Inverness (covering all lines north of Dunblane and north and west of Crianlarich) formed the only intermediate level of management. Inverness's 'Highland Lines' office was semi-autonomous, responsible for every aspect of management until closure of branches, and of the lines between Aviemore, Forres and Elgin, led to its disbanding in 1967 and effective relegation to a district office. From November 1969 the two-tier reform was complete, with 65 area/depot area managers reporting to divisional or HQ officers. Scotland's biggest commercial office building, Buchanan House, was opened in November 1969 where Buchanan Street Station's carriage sidings had once been, as Regional HQ to house 2,000 staff.

A New Outlook

A new outlook from the Marples-Beeching period became evident in 1968, with the appointment of Barbara Castle as Minister of Transport in a Labour government. Every change of government was marked by a new Transport Act, and that of 1968 marked a crucial new step in the political management of railways in Britain. It made provision for subsidising selected railway services for social reasons. These would receive grants, for specific periods of time, to keep them running. Twenty years before, the LMS and LNER had proudly claimed that Britain's railways had never required a subsidy. The maximum period of grants initially was three years, and among the Scottish routes to be supported were Glasgow-Perth-Inverness (£294,000), Glasgow-Dundee (£249,000), and Aberdeen-Inverness (£290,000), sums eclipsed by grants to the Glasgow North and Glasgow South electric systems, of £1,445,000 and £1,051,000 respectively in 1969. In 1969-70, £9,463,000 of subsidy went to maintain 30 Scottish routes. The Act also wrote off much of BR's very large capital debt. In order to focus on the transport needs of large conurbations, passenger transport authorities were to be set up (not in Scotland at this time). The railway freight business was also addressed, with British Railways' loss-making sundries-carrying business hived off to a new entity, the National Freight Corporation, along with the Freightliner container service. Ships, hotels and property management remained responsibilities of the British Railways Board. This last item was a very important one: disposal of redundant land and buildings brought in millions of pounds.

Scotland's last railway hotel opened at St. Andrews in June 1968, built on the site of the one-time goods station. The town lost its railway in January 1969. Scottish railways had once built stations for their hotels, as at Turnberry and Gleneagles – now a hotel was built where a railway was being shut down. The hotel was, however, the responsibility not of Scottish Region, but the British Transport Hotels Division, of which W.G. Thorpe, regional general manager from 1963 to 1967, was a director.

Class A4 60031 *Golden Plover* on an Aberdeen-Glasgow train at Perth, c1963. The window of the tender corridor can be seen. From 1962 to 1965 it was based at St. Rollox depot. (North British Railway Study Group)

The Gradual Reinvention of British Railways – the 1970s and 80s

No More Cuts (Almost)

A significant late closure was the line between Kinross and Perth (Bridge of Earn) in Spring 1970. Not a Beeching cut, this appeared to have been at government instigation in order to use part of the trackbed for the new M90 motorway. Services from Edinburgh to Perth and the Highlands had to be redirected by Larbert and Stirling. In 1975 the Ladybank-Bridge of Earn railway, which had lost its passenger traffic in 1955, had it restored to provide a somewhat more direct route. Thirty-six stations lost their freight traffic that year, mostly in the Edinburgh and Glasgow districts, with nine in the Highlands. But passenger line closures virtually ceased. Political rather than operational reasons were responsible. When the BRB identified the Further North, Kyle, West Highland and Oban lines to the Ministry of Transport as suitable candidates for closure in 1974 and 1975 (possibly headquarters-inspired rather than a regional initiative) neither a Labour government nor its Conservative successor made any move to shut them down.

After the events of the 1960s, the 1970s, if less tumultuous, continued to offer plenty of challenges to a team which, one assumes, was by now attuned to crisis management. General managers came and went: four within the decade, and other senior staff were often transferred from Region to HQ or another region, under a well-established BTC policy designed to avoid personal fiefdoms, but which at least gave its executives experience of the whole system.

A Wick-Inverness train drawn by a Class 37 in BR 1970s blue livery passes the closed station of The Mound, where the platform for the Dornoch branch (closed 1960) was still visible. (Stenlake Collection)

An Dundee-Edinburgh Class 105 diesel unit pauses in 1970 at Barry Links, a station built in 1838 and enlarged by 1903 to serve the adjacent military camp. The building on the one-time island platform has since been demolished. (Stenlake Collection)

The two-tier refocusing of management helped to keep traffic figures up: Scottish freight tonnage in 1969 was 21.1 million tons, compared with 21.4 million tons in 1966, and receipts were £20 million against £22.6 million (of the 1969 figure over 30% came from coal, and 20% from iron and steel). New car factories at Bathgate and Linwood, and new steel works at Motherwell and Glengarnock, promised new freight traffic. Just as coal production was shrinking, proving of North Sea oil deposits began, and Scotland was found to have large off-shore reserves. Exploitation of these brought some regeneration to the northern lines' declining freight traffic, with haulage of pipe sections and other construction materials, and a proposal for singling of the Aberdeen line between Montrose and Stonehaven was dropped. But the rails between Maud Junction and Peterhead were lifted before the oil industry got under way, and oil traffic was not enough to prevent the complete closure of the Fraserburgh line in 1979.

At the end of the 70s a new freight route was established with the opening of the Hunterston deep water terminal, from where imported ore was taken in the heaviest freight trains seen in Scotland, 2,100 tonnes, to the huge new steel works and strip mill at Ravenscraig. Operating efficiency was raised with the introduction in Scotland of TOPS (total operations processing system: enthusiasm for acronyms was growing fast) in 1975 for control of wagon stocks, with locomotives added in 1977 and passenger coaches in 1983. Another notable event was completion of electrification of the West Coast Main Line into Glasgow Central, on 6 May 1974. New Class 87 electric locomotives with a continuous rating of 5000hp could pull 500-ton trains at speeds of up to 100 mph. On this route, for the first time, standard class carriages had air-conditioning.

A Greater Glasgow Trans-Clyde electric train at Balloch Pier Station, 1981. (Stenlake Collection)

The Strathclyde PTA, and a New Sector for Scottish Region

Having done its own restructuring in the 1960s, the region largely escaped the BRB's unfortunate attempt to reorganise its operations through the 'Field' system devised at enormous expense by the McKinsey management consultancy, and abandoned in 1975. In 1973 a new partnership was formed, when the Greater Glasgow Passenger Transport Authority was established. Renamed the Strathclyde Passenger Transport Authority (SPTA), this body took responsibility for transport throughout the newly-formed Strathclyde region, in 1975. Its executive arm, the SPTE, operated Glasgow city buses and the Subway, and provided co-ordination of Scottish Bus Group, British Rail and Cal-Mac steamer services. It had an interest in more than half of the Scottish Region's business, and – crucially – held the purse-strings of public subsidy.

Existence of PTAs, with their need to know what they were paying for, was one of the factors that impelled the BR board, under the chairmanship of Sir Peter Parker, to divide its passenger business from 1977 into four cost and revenue centres: InterCity, London & South East, PTA Services, and Other Provincial Services. All Scottish Region trains apart from the Strathclyde regional network fell into the last category, with its far from uplifting name. For Parker and Bob Reid, the board member for marketing (who had had a succession of managerial roles in Scottish Region from 1960 to 1968), this was a step towards a much more substantial change. Made BR's chief executive from 1980, Reid introduced a further restructuring in January 1982. From Nationalisation and before, there had been a vertically-arranged command structure, with central officers in charge of major functions passing orders to regions which themselves were similarly organised. Now five market sectors were formed, each with its own director and separately accountable for profit or loss. These were InterCity, Rail Express Systems (parcels, mail, newspapers), Provincial Services (regional and inter-regional passenger services), London & South East (later Network Southeast), Trainload Freight, and Railfreight Distribution. Parker and Reid chose to superimpose the sectors on the regional structure, and a complex 'matrix' format ensued, with regional general managers, sector directors and functional chiefs all at the same level, and reporting to the chief executive. Reid became chairman on Parker's departure in 1983. His matrix model, with its potentially conflicting lines of command, has been seen as a device to promote change without prompting interference by the Ministry of Transport in what was effectively a reorganisation. Everyone in the railway knew the real new controllers were the sector directors.

Scotland was something of an exception. Although in theory the Director of Provincial Services (not a title likely to win friends in Scotland) had control of all Scottish Region train services, regional management, with the tacit support of BRB's chief executive, was taking the future into its own hands. Central to this was a new arrival from London HQ, Chris Green, as chief operating manager from 1980 and deputy general manager from 1983. After the success of the Two-Tier reorganisation, Scottish management had not maintained innovation through the 1970s. Certain things had been achieved. With the M8 motorway partly open even before final completion in 1980, passenger numbers on the Glasgow-Edinburgh route began to fall, and a speed-up was implemented, using locomotive-hauled trains with a Class 27 diesel at each end. These were not successful and were replaced in late 1979 by a high-punctuality 45-minute service using push-pull trains with the latest Mark III carriages, a powerful Class 47 locomotive, and a brake van fitted with a driving cab. Glasgow's cross-city line passing under Central Station, one of the Beeching closures, was reinstated with electric traction in November 1979, and renamed the Argyle Line, with trains initially between Dumbarton and Motherwell. Many stations remained drab and cheerless, however, and the operational focus was on running trains for the public to use, rather than on how to get the public to use the trains.

Signs of Independence: the Invention of ScotRail
Green identified three immediate crisis issues: the coming deregulation of inter-city coach services, the relationship with Strathclyde PTE, and the BRB's proposal to make further cuts including the Kyle, Oban, Ardrossan/Largs and North Berwick lines. The Regional team now embarked on a programme which in effect treated the Scottish system as an integral unit. To win back passenger numbers in the face of new and ruthless road competition, Green insisted that passengers' total experience of their railway journey had to be catered for, from entry to a smart station to punctual arrival in a clean, comfortable and up-to-date train. His messages to operating staff were clear, specific, and often took them into his confidence. Detailed regional plans were introduced from 1981, setting out a range of targets and how they would be achieved, from train-cleaning to freight train punctuality and better station services. Combating competition from overnight coaches, a 'Nightrider' service in 1982 from Glasgow and Edinburgh to London offered first class (non-sleeper) carriages at the attractive fare of £17. For internal services a new basic-interval timetable was introduced, based on Swiss practice, with regular-interval connections to ease journey planning, and a speeding-up of many trains.

What was happening was just what Hurcomb and Robertson had sought to prevent, but things were different in the 1980s. The culmination was the re-branding of BR (Scottish Region) as Scotrail (changed soon to ScotRail), in September 1983. The chosen name was a brilliant one, national, modern, clear and memorable. In 1984 Green was made general manager, evidence that BR HQ did not look unfavourably on the Scottish initiatives. It seemed that in Scotland at least, regional tradition and identity could be successfully fused with the dynamic, market-oriented, sectorised approach in tackling railway management.

The SPTA was concerned about the increasing gulf between revenues and operating costs in the train services it supported. Asbestos removal from its Class 303 'Blue Trains' was a major expense. In 1983 it had to provide £28.9 million of subsidy, more than three times the 1976 figure (though inflation played a part). It had withdrawn support in 1981 from the Glasgow-Paisley (Canal)-Kilmacolm line, which was closed in January 1983. A ScotRail initiative led to a a joint planning group, which eventually agreed on a strategy combining cost-reduction, modernisation and operating efficiency, intended to bring down the subsidy to £18.6 million by 1988. By no means a purely negative programme, it included electrification to Ayr, Ardrossan and Largs, and the reopening of the line to Paisley (Canal). Deregulation of all bus services from October 1986 and their removal from PTE control helped to focus the SPTA's attention on the railways. A new drive for collaboration with other local authorities resulted in station improvements across the country and the restoration of trains between Edinburgh and Bathgate, in March 1986. Carrying double the anticipated number of passengers, this line confirmed a new, positive sense of the railway as a community asset.

One of the striking things about the Scottish Region's self re-invention was that it was achieved by its own management. Like other very large organisations, the BRB had a tendency to hire consultants to advise it on on how to organise its own activities (though they were sometimes wished upon it by the government, or employed in the hope of justifying rail policy to the government). One government initiative of 1982-83 was an inquiry into British Railways' financial position and prospects, by a small team under Sir David Serpell, a former civil servant who had worked with Beeching in the 1960s, and had been a BRB director since 1974. Their report in January 1983 gave a detailed and critical analysis of the BRB's accounts and financial projections before setting out a series of options for a future national railway system. While making no specific recommendations, it gave equal weight, among other options, to the proposition that Great Britain could get by almost without railways at all, and that all Scotland needed was the West Coast Main Line to Glasgow and Edinburgh: nothing else. Shades of 1841! Feebly and briefly defended by the Minister of Transport, the report was very quickly shelved. Railway managers, however, found it contained much useful information for planning purposes.

New Working Methods and Old-Type Industrial Relations

The creation of ScotRail was an immediate success with the public, the media, and, importantly, the staff. Nevertheless, the campaign to build public esteem had to contend with a succession of industrial disputes. Through the 1970s railway wages had risen less than other industries' and though a 20% increase and a reduction in the working week from 40 to 39 hours was offered in 1980, this barely matched price inflation, and industrial relations across all BR regions and sectors remained troubled, with Scotland no exception. In mid-1982 the ASLEF union mounted a strike against British Rail's plan for flexible rostering (meaning some longer shifts within the overall working week) which ended only when the British Railways Board threatened to sack the strikers. At the same time, another headqurters initiative, an "open stations" programme, was being trialled in Scotland (the relatively self-contained nature of the Region's system made it a favoured place for try-outs). No more queues at ticket gates: instead tickets were inspected on the trains by a conductor. Public reaction was mixed, with passenger complaints going up by 19% in 1982-83. One of the intentions was to reduce the possibility of fraudulent travel, estimated to cost the railways many millions each year. Another

A Class 47 with a Perth-Inverness train stops at Blair Atholl, 1984. (Stenlake Collection)

was to improve workers' productivity, and this led to long and difficult talks with the National Union of Railwaymen.

In 1983 the NUR elected a new general secretary in Jimmy Knapp, a Scot from the ranks of the signalmen, born in the Ayrshire railway community of Hurlford. Described by one reporter as "six foot two of Scottish socialist", Knapp was a tough negotiator who matched the new, robust attitude of the management, (with its insistence on productivity deals), and also proved successful at keeping public opinion on the railway workers' side even when successive one-day strikes were disrupting everyone's travel plans. The key issue was the abolition of guards on commuter trains, where their prime duty was to open and close the doors, and their partial replacement by conductors whose main function would be ticket inspection, while the doors were operated by the driver. Some trains might have only a driver on board, known as DOO (driver-only operation). This was hotly resisted by the NUR, citing passenger safety as a main concern. The 'Strathclyde Manning Agreement' was established in 1985, which permitted DOO trains on the Strathclyde lines, on the understanding that a ticket inspector would also, normally, be on the train. Still, implementation was gradual, and other issues remained, or would arise. The 1981 Operating Plan had noted that "Scottish Region Establishments are inflated by the heavy sickness and absenteeism that all industries face in Western Scotland". Even with real staff enthusiasm for the ScotRail identity, the conflicting priorities of unions and management would ensure that "progress" had more than one definition.

A Success Story

From 1984 to 1990 a programme of expansion and modernisation went ahead on ScotRail's territory. The threat to rural lines was averted by 'Operation Phoenix': between 1984 and 1988, on the Kyle, Wick/Thurso, Mallaig and Oban lines, where conventional signalling was replaced by the radio electric token block (RETB) system with a substantial saving of costs. The resolve of the management to keep the Far North lines going may have been tested by the collapse of the Ness Viaduct at Inverness in February 1989, but the decision to rebuild it was quickly made. In other ways ingenuity made up for limitations on investment. Scottish Region engineers at Glasgow Works (the former St. Rollox) devised a control system for the push-pull expresses using the train's electric lighting circuit between driving cab and locomotive. The Fort William-London sleeper service, threatened with closure in 1983 because the West Highland line's Class 37 engines were not fitted for electric heating as needed by the new Mark III sleeping cars, was rescued by the conversion at Inverurie of old Class 25 engines into ETHELs (electric train heating ex-locomotives), their generators providing the necessary power. From 1984 steam came back to the Mallaig line with well-patronised summer excursions. As a hopeful indicator of things to come, in the early 1980s British Rail's high-speed tilting Advanced Passenger Train prototype made occasional runs into Scotland; in October 1981 it was recorded as going south from Beattock Summit at 125 mph, a speed which has not been equalled since, and on 12 December 1984 it ran from Euston to Glasgow Central in 3 hours, 52 minutes and 40 seconds, at an average speed of 103 mph. Hopes for it were very high: Scottish Region had bid for 60 APT sets, but mounting costs and technical problems caused the project's abandonment in 1986.

Green was whisked south in 1986 to tackle the even greater challenge of Network Southeast, but by then ScotRail was well-launched and confident, with

Dumbarton Central, prior to restoration and refurbishment, with a Class 303 unit forming an Airdrie train. (Stenlake Collection)

managers and staff who took to heart his dictum that quality of service must be the vital theme. It successfully resisted acquiring the bus-type 'Pacer' diesel units favoured by Provincial management, preferring to use locomotive-hauled trains on longer non-electrified routes. In the interest of co-ordination and a new flexibility of approach, the number of area managers was cut from eleven to four in 1988. Route business management was applied to the prime interurban lines and the Fife commuter services, with a brief taking in service specifications, fares, quality standards, competition, and staff morale. By the early 1990s a "Changing Face of ScotRail" promotional pamphlet could record that "The Scottish Region staff rallied under the ScotRail banner", and add with some pride that "All staff in contact with customers have had at least one charm school session."

Changing Trends in the ScotRail Era

Changing trends in freight and passenger traffic emerge from a comparison of 1980 and 1984 figures. In 1980 Scottish Region carried 24.4 million tonnes of freight for receipts of £34.3 million; in 1984 the tonnage was 11.9 million and the receipts £23.7 million. One million tonnes of coal were carried, against six million tonnes in 1980. The number of passenger journeys in 1980 was 61.5 million, with receipts of £81.4 million. In 1984 the number of journeys had fallen to 52 million though receipts rose to £91.7 million. While freight volumes would continue to decline, however, passenger traffic was on the point of a sustained rise.

Margaret Thatcher began a second term as prime minister in 1983. Among her ministers and advisers, the concept of railway privatisation always simmered. There were obvious problems – how to sell off an industry whose survival depended on large amounts of public money being regularly pumped into it might challenge the most determined free marketeer. But there was one obvious way to make a start, by identifying parts which could be detached and profitably sold off. This process had really begun in the 1960s with the sale of sale of redundant sites and disused equipment, but that had brought income to British Railways. In the new process, the beneficiary was Her Majesty's Treasury, starting in 1984 with the disposal of British Transport Hotels. Sectorisation unintentionally also encouraged the prospect of privatisation, making it easier to identify the 'commercial' and the 'social' railways.

After the bouncy years of the 1970s, the 1980s until their final year were a decade of economic growth, with InterCity and Railfreight Distribution (a 1988 amalgamation of Freightliners, the Speedlink wagonload service and Railfreight International) both showing a profit. This was partly due to a retrenchment of services which had not been profitable: general collection and delivery of goods ceased in 1981, Royal Mail parcels by rail ended in 1986, and newspaper traffic switched to the roads in 1988.

In 1985 ScotRail was operating 277 main line diesel locomotives, though the numbers would soon dwindle rapidly as more substantial and reliable diesel unit types became available in the form of the Class 156 "Super Sprinters" from 1987, and particularly the Class 158 90 mph "Express Sprinters" from late 1990. Also in 1985 there were 64 Class 08 diesel shunters, nineteen Class 81 electric locomotives, 43 HST power cars, 106 electric and 86 diesel multiple units. Of the 457 passenger carriages, 147 were of British Railways Mark I type from the 1950s-60s, 249 were Mark II (1964-75) and 32 were Mk IIIa (1975-88).

A Privatised Railway

British Rail's Achievement

In 1990 Sir Bob Reid retired as British Railway Board chairman, to be replaced by his namesake Sir Bob Reid (railway students refer to Bob Reid I and Bob Reid II). The new chairman was a Scot, born in Cupar, with a successful career in the oil industry. His prime task, though he did not know it at first, would be to preside over the break-up of British Railways, though he was not responsible for the chosen form of disposal. British Rail had gradually risen from the low point reached in the 60s and 70s to a stage in which it was generally seen as efficient and providing a good public service. ScotRail had run ahead of it, its new *esprit de corps* helping towards a higher level of punctuality and of customer approval than the majority of regions. Apart from its relatively early adoption of a marketing approach focused on customer needs and wishes, other factors may have played a part. Preservation of the lines to the northern and western extremities helped to give the system a national character, rather than merely that of a transit operation for high-density traffic. The re-instatement of lines and stations closed only a decade or two before was another positive aspect. Stations were smartened up and even those which were unstaffed and provided only with bus-shelter type refuges from the weather had information screens and train arrival announcements. Also, as the public became more educated in, and more aware of, the vulnerability of the 'natural' environment, railways were seen as environmentally friendlier than road traffic (even if the response on carrying bicycles was somewhat grudging). If the railways were on a roll, though, it was by their own efforts both in the back-rooms, where sector requirements and regional provision were sorted out; and in the new-look stations where staff were being trained to understand and respond to customers' needs. Some people disliked the

SPTA electric train at Cathcart Station, 1991. (Stenlake Collection)

idea of a passenger being a 'customer' but it reminded railway staff that people paid for the service, and very often could choose an alternative.

In mileage terms, ScotRail was the largest of the five Regional Railways with 1,674 route miles and the second-largest number of stations, at 311. Between 1985 and 1994, 69 had been opened, almost half as many as in England during the same period, 36 of them in the SPTA area. ScotRail was moved further in the direction of self-management by being made (from 1991) a separate profit centre within Regional Railways as part of the BRB's latest and last organisational reform. Styled 'Organising for Quality' (OfQ), it built on sectorisation by creating nine business units as profit centres, or groups of profit centres. A key point was that these units became the owners of their own assets, and were expected to trade among themselves for the use of these assets: thus InterCity would buy use of ScotRail track and stations for its through trains from and to England. Criticised by some as a preparatory move to ease privatisation, it was in fact part of a BRB drive to make the railways more profit-conscious and to minimise their dependence on public subsidy, at a time when privatisation was a government option rather than a firm policy. Cyril Bleasdale, Scottish Region's general manager from 1990-94, was also provincial manager of ScotRail.

September 1990 saw the introduction of the 90 mph Class 158 Express Sprinter diesel trains, intended first of all for the Edinburgh-Aberdeen route, but unfortunately beset by the teething troubles that still seemed almost inevitable with new traction. With the problems resolved, they became popular with travellers. In May 1991, a pair of 158s made the Waverley-Queen Street run in 32 minutes 9 seconds at an average 88 mph, with maxima of 107 mph. In 1990-91 the North Berwick branch was electrified and the line between Glasgow Central and Paisley (Canal) reopened. Two collisions, at Bellgrove in 1989 and Newton in 1990, both at junctions where double track was reduced to 'single lead', with two and four deaths respectively, caused rethinking and eventual restoration of 'double lead' at busy junctions. ScotRail produced a positive marketing plan for 1992-93 with targeted revenue increases on its four designated route types, Express (up 13%), Long Urban (up 3.1%), Short Urban (up 5.1%) and Rural (up 6.3%). From the evidence of growing usage, ScotRail was generally doing what its users wanted.With an irony that seemed to govern all three 20th century re-arrangements of the railways, just as a form of state ownership that worked well – cost-conscious, customer-oriented, seeking profits where they could be made – had been established, it would be broken up to conform with a different political-economic philosophy.

Preparation for Privatisation

A Conservative government under John Major was re-elected in 1992. In Scotland Labour won 49 seats, the Conservatives 11, the Liberal Democrats 9, and the SNP 3. Railway privatisation was part of the new government's programme, though a majority of Scottish electors had not voted for it. Two Scots, however, served as successive ministers of transport in the run-up to privatisation, Malcolm Rifkind (1990-92) and John MacGregor (1992-94). Rifkind had favoured privatisation of the existing set-up, but MacGregor's brief was for a single corporation (set up as Railtrack) as permanent owner of track, stations and all installations, and 27 route operators on fixed-term franchises granted by a semi-independent franchise director. After a lapse of 70 years, the concept of competition was once again invoked in railway service, since some train operators would be sharing lines. The Railways Act of 1993 cleared the line for British Railways to be disposed of. With an annual turnover reckoned at £200 million, of which £87 million came from fares and £130 million fom subsidy, ScotRail was chosen as one of the first seven 'model franchises'. Managing it as a shadow franchise required trimming its costs to make it a more attractive package to bidders. Pressure to shed staff was resisted, but routine maintenance work came virtually to a halt. In 1993 Bleasdale had to impose a 'maintenance holiday' decreed by Regional Railways HQ as part of a 20% spending reduction. Painting of the Forth Bridge, famously a continuous task, was halted for a year, and the painters redeployed.

Two new bodies were set up to manage privatisation. The Office of Rail Regulation (ORR), independent of the government, was to ensure that new train operating companies followed the franchise terms and also to look after the interests of passengers. The Office of Passenger Rail Franchising (OPRAF) was responsible to the government for overseeing the terms of franchises and subsidies – it was accepted that most franchises would be impossible to lease out without a system of subsidy in place to preserve services unprofitable in themselves but considered socially essential. Three new companies were formed to take over ownership of all passenger trains and locomotives, which would be leased to franchise holders. Bidders had to calculate the elements of revenue from services and subsidy, and balance these against the costs of providing the stipulated level of service, including stock leasing charges and payments to the infrastructure company, in order to make a bid which also assured their own required profit margin. Railtrack, rolling stock companies and franchise holders were all supposed to make a profit.

In 1993 excitement arose around the potential of the Channel Tunnel to give Scotland better access to European markets. Indeed, trans-Tunnel sleepers from Glasgow and Edinburgh had been planned (and the cars built at a cost of £150 million) though the services never materialised. When the Tunnel opened in May 1994, a link service from Edinburgh to London Waterloo was started, but little used, and was withdrawn in January 1997.

Bleasdale retired on 31 March 1994 and on 1 April ScotRail was made a separate entity as a division of the British Railways Board. Chris Green returned as its Director, with the aim of mounting a management buy-out. At the same time the new Railtrack company took control of track and signalling. Controversy erupted in March 1995 when ScotRail, newly given responsibility for the Anglo-Scottish sleepers, proposed to close the London-Fort William service, at the behest of Roger Salmon, the franchise director. Not for the first time, war-cries from the Highlands disrupted plans made in London. The Court of Session ruled that the full procedures for a closure proposal must be followed, and the scheme was eventually dropped. Green resigned in April 1995, discouraged by the prospect of more enforced cuts to Scottish services, which conflicted with his plans for enhancement. He was succeeded by John Ellis, a keen privatiser, who also hoped to lead a management buyout. In December 1995 the ScotRail business and most of the old Scottish Region's assets and liabilities were vested in ScotRail Railways Ltd, a wholly-owned subsidiary of the BRB, set up as a vehicle for the privatisation process.

Chris Green in 1994, Director of ScotRail. (ScotRail News)

Painters are at work as a Carlisle-bound Class 156 Sprinter enters Sanquhar Station. It is one of around 200 stations supported by a community organisation, in this case the Brighten Up Sanquhar Group. (Stenlake Collection)

The ScotRail Franchise: National Express Takes Over

In the year to 31 March 1996, ScotRail earned £71.9 million, and carried 49 million passengers, at an operating cost of £323.9 million, of which £170 million was paid to Railtrack. It employed 3,977 people, and received subsidies totalling £251 million. During 1996 and into 1997, there was considerable disruption and loss of income from strikes mounted by the RMT Union (formed in 1990 from the NUR and the National Union of Seamen) in protest against productivity demands made on guards and conductors. In that year the Health & Safety Executive required Railtrack to start emergency work on the Forth Bridge or face prosecution – painting had been in abeyance for three years. New techniques of shot-blast and oxide paint were now to last for 25 years.

Despite being selected as an early candidate for privatisation, ScotRail was almost the last to be sold off. The reason was external: Scottish local authorities had been reorganised from April 1996, replacing the region and district arrangement of 1975 with unitary authorities. The Strathclyde Region was broken into twelve authorities, and the Strathclyde Passenger Transport Authority had to be recast to take account of this. Most of these authorities were Labour-controlled and not happy about a profit-making company receiving public money to the tune of £105,568,000 to run their trains. Also the PTA wanted its full timetable of 520 routes to be protected by inclusion in the franchise terms. By February 1997 all the issues were resolved, and National Express was named preferred bidder, beating the managemenent buy-out led by Ellis and three other bids including one from the Scottish-based Stagecoach bus company. The contract was for seven years, with a built-in subsidy of £280.1 million in 1997-98, dropping to £202 million in 2003-04. National Express committed itself to running no less than the current number of train miles and to provide enhancements to services and stations. The new franchise holder was also Scotland's largest bus operator, owner of Scottish CityLink coaches which since 1988 had been competing vigorously with the trains. This led to the franchise deal being referred to the Monopolies & Mergers Commission, which required National Express to divest itself of Scottish CityLink within six months.

After almost fifty years, the Scottish railway system entered a new phase of ownership and control. In the half century since Nationalisation, there had been plenty of change. A Rip van Winkle from 1948 would have recognised much in the way of architecture, and semaphore signals still in many places, but little else would seem familiar. Some lines, like the Callander & Oban as far as Crianlarich, or from Dumfries to Stranraer, or those that once passed by such places as Muirkirk, Maud, Forfar, or Crieff, were taking on the appearance of archaeological remains like the earthworks of the old North Britons. But shiny electric trains running under central Glasgow, local stations without staff but equipped with electronic screens and disembodied voices providing train information, power signal boxes controlling many miles, electric trains running from Edinburgh to London in four hours, fast trainloads of containers with no brake van, would have seemed a vision of the far future come true. It was a reduced network, 1,894 miles (3,030 km) compared with the 3,730 miles (5,968 km) left by the LMS and LNER, but clearly still an essential element in national life.

Three other train companies (TOCs) ran services into Scotland: Great North Eastern Railway to Edinburgh, with limited services to Glasgow, Aberdeen and Inverness; Cross-Country from south west England to Edinburgh, Glasgow and Aberdeen, and West Coast Trains between London and Glasgow via Lockerbie; the last two both owned by the Virgin Group. None required a Scottish subsidy, and competition with ScotRail was minimal (ScotRail did not run trains between Edinburgh and Berwick, and Dunbar was a GNER station). The years between 1997 and 2000 were not good for the owners and users of privatised railways, even though passenger numbers rose. In a book focused on the Scottish system it can only be noted in passing that the attempt to have 25 train operating franchises was a failure, with punctuality declining and costs rising. In the next round the number of franchises would be fewer. Railtrack, floated on the Stock Exchange in 1996, and seen to be focused more on delivering shareholder results than infrastructure maintenance, lost an increasingly battered reputation for effective management with the Hatfield accident of 17 October 2000 and the resultant panic imposition of hundreds of speed restrictions and temporary line closures, including the West Coast Main Line north of Carlisle for three days. In September 2001 Railtrack was placed in administration by the government and a new 'not-for-profit' state-owned company, Network Rail, replaced it from October 2002. Its Scottish office was run by a local director. Other changes came as government grappled with the problems arising from the first privatisations. The (Labour) government abolished the Office of Passenger Rail Franchise and set up the Strategic Rail Authority (SRA) in its place, with a brief to exercise tighter control on franchise grants and to monitor the train companies more closely. The independent Office of Rail Regulation became the Office of Rail and Road in July 2004.

In Scotland a Rail Partnership programme between the railway operators and local authorities was formed, with schemes including "Edinburgh crossrail" and development of the Invernet system around Inverness. The SRA published a strategic plan in 2002, which included the provision of rail links to Glasgow and Edinburgh Airports by 2010, but in a revision of 2003, these projects were downgraded to "being studied" (Edinburgh Airport's rail connection is now by tram from the new Edinburgh Gateway Station, while Glasgow Airport's was still undecided by mid-2017). National Express found the ScotRail business leaner than it had expected (its Managing Director acknowledged in 2002 that the BR men "knew

A panoramic view of the modernised station at Stirling with its new canopies, completed in May 2016. (Derek MacLeod Contruction Ltd)

how to squeeze a pound") but it maintained a high ranking in performance standards, coming second in total performance in 1998, with 95.9% punctuality (arrival on time or within ten minutes) and 99.4% 'reliability'. In the first two years of privatisation, its passenger journeys rose by 11%. From 2000, after the establishment of the Scottish Parliament and Executive, the company subtitled itself 'Scotland's National Railway'. In 2002 it ran into financial trouble, primarily with its Central Trains franchise in England, and a £115 million loss was forecast. In a restructuring of the franchise agreement, the subsidy for 2003-04 went up by £54 million. Under Peter Cotton as managing director great efforts were made from 2002, and by 2004 the franchise had a list of achievements to chalk up, of which some would only be completed in the next incarnation of ScotRail. It provided a new train servicing facility at Eastfield in late 2004, introduced 74 new multiple-unit trains, 27 more than the franchise commitment, opened eight new stations, introduced the 15-minute interval Edinburgh-Glasgow service, maintained above-average records of punctuality and customer satisfaction, and was named UK Rail Operator of the Year in 2004. Its essential failure was its inability to achieve the necessary level of profitability. To match the original proposed subsidy reductions, it needed to effect an improvement of 10% a year but only managed 0.4% in 1998-99 and 1999-2000, and a loss was incurred in the other years between 1997 and 2004.

West Coast, East Coast, and Freight Services

The West and East Coast cross-border franchises had mixed fortunes. Twenty years after the APT experiments, completion of the West Coast Main Line modernisation in December 2005 allowed Virgin Railways to use a development of APT tilting technology on its Italian-built Pendolino trains, which had been running on the West Coast Main Line since January 2004. Originally estimated at £2.5 billion, then alarmingly re-forecast at £14.5 billion, the ultimate cost after Network Rail got a firm grip on the project was £8.6 billion. Glasgow to London in 4½ hours was now a standard, and fears were already being expressed that the line would have insufficient capacity as early as 2015 if the levels of traffic growth seen in 2005-06 were maintained. The prospect of an extension into Scotland of the HS2 project was being aired, giving three-hour timings to London. In 2012 the next franchise was awarded to First Group, but Virgin contested the evaluation process, and after a legal battle with the Department for Transport, regained it for the next fifteen years. The East Coast Main Line also underwent a saga. Great North Eastern Railway, a vehicle of Sea Containers plc, was the first franchisee, for seven years from 1996, extended to April 2005. With GNER in financial straits, the government withdrew the franchise and GNER ran the line on a fixed-fee basis until National Express became the new franchise holder in 2007. National Express in turn defaulted on its agreement in July 2009, and from November the trains were run as East Coast Trains, a subsidiary of the state-owned Directly Owned Railways, a safety net for such emergencies. East Coast Trains ran the franchise very successfully until February 2015, when a new commercial franchise was agreed with Virgin Trains East Coast, a body owned 10% by Virgin Trains and 90% by Stagecoach.

Privatised freight services were organised on a quite separate basis. There were no franchises and the companies which acquired the various parts of British Rail's freight business owned their own rolling stock or used customers' wagons. The new freight companies, all English-based, obtained access to Scottish routes from Railtrack and set up their own depots. The largest operator, English, Welsh & Scottish Railways, was a subsidiary of the (American) Wisconsin Railroad company, subsequently sold and now German-owned as DB Cargo. Other operators, Colas Rail, Freightliner, GB Railfreight and Direct Rail Services (state-owned and originally set up to transport nuclear waste) also ran services based on container operations and bulk loads. Freight trains from Scotland to Europe via the Channel Tunnel had been forecast in 1993, though they did not come about. At Mossend, near Bellshill, a European freight terminal was laid out, now Mossend International Freight Park. The Gushetfaulds freightliner terminal was shut down in 1993, its traffic relocated to Mossend and Freightliner's intermodal terminal at Coatbridge, which had opened in 1968. Coal remained a substantial element in the freight market, and the port at Hunterston, no longer handling iron ore after the closure of Ravenscraig Steel Works in 1992, found a new role in importing coal, carried forward by rail to the huge power station at Longannet (closed in 2016). Railtrack's difficulties and the delays in modernising the West Coast Main Line discouraged

Shirley is one of many woman conductors. ScotRail also employs around 60 woman drivers. (ScotRail)

development of freight traffic and it was not until the Scottish Executive was enabled to set up Transport Scotland in 2005, in order to manage all aspects of government responsibility for all modes of transport, that the question of rail freight was given serious attention. An important issue was that of loading gauge. The largest rail-borne containers were now 9ft 6in high and 2.6 metres wide (Gauge W12), too big to fit on many lines built to 19th century clearances. Apart from the West Coast Main Line, able to take Gauge W10, 9ft 6in high by 2.5 metres wide, most Scottish lines were restricted to the 9ft high W9 gauge. Priority routes for upgrading were identified as Mossend-Aberdeen-Elgin, Gretna-Mossend (West Coast Main Line), Hunterston-Mossend and Coatbridge, with extended or dynamic (two-way running) loops on the Gretna-Dumfries-Kilmarnock, Ayr-Mossend and Perth-Inverness lines, for trains 775 metres long.

A Transport Scotland document, *Delivering the Goods: Scotland's Rail Freight Strategy* was published in early 2016. Acknowledging the steep decline in coal and steel traffic, it stressed the need to exploit smaller markets for the 44 freight railheads and eleven intermodal terminals. The £30 million Scottish Rail Freight Investment Fund was available for such purposes as day-to-day operation of the rail network, new lines, and additional gauge clearance. A Joint Freight Board, set up in 2012, was asked to explore ways of overcoming barriers to innovation. The commitment to rail freight development is closely linked to European Union targets for modal shift from road to rail/water by 30% in 2030 and 50% in 2050 (for distances over 300km). To achieve that in Scotland will not be easy.

Transport Scotland and the Second Franchise: First ScotRail

From 2000, the Scottish Executive was involved in placing the franchise of 2004, though the Strategic Rail Authority controlled the process. It was won by another transport empire that had begun as a bus company, the Aberdeen-based First Group, which took over on 17 October. First ScotRail's managing director was Mary Dickson, the first woman to head a Scottish railway company. The SRA's responsibilities for Scotland were transferred to the Scottish Executive in August-October 2005, which set up the Transport Scotland agency to manage them. Transport Scotland's Railway Directorate was charged with supervision of the ScotRail franchise and decreed in 2008 that the ScotRail name and the "saltire" livery of the trains was to be maintained irrespective of who held the franchise, thus assuring a continuing national identity across the system, including the Strathclyde trains, which previously had their own livery. The SPTA was reformed into the Strathclyde Partnership for Transport (SPT), with responsibility for transport co-ordination and planning, but no financial involvement with or operational control of railways. Similar bodies were set up in the Highlands, North East, Tayside and Central, South East and South West regions. Another new organisation was Passenger Focus Scotland, a "consumer watchdog" to speak for and protect the interest of rail travellers, though without specific powers.

With passenger journeys continuing to rise, from 63,690,000 in 2004-05 to 80,175,000 in 2008-9, First ScotRail had to face many complaints about overcrowding in the first years. Even so, customer satisfaction remained above the UK average. A Passenger Focus report in Autumn 2008 recorded that from spring 2004 approval level never went below 83% and in one year reached 91% against a UK average ranging from 73% to 83% – though only 42% in that period thought that First ScotRail dealt adequately with the specific problem of delays. When Mary Dickson (now Grant) left the company in 2011, operations director Steve Montgomery became managing director. There had been political controversy in 2008 over how a three-year extension of the franchise to 2015 had been handled, and a low point in May 2012 when Montgomery joined with his Network Rail counterpart, David Simpson, to apologise for poor service in the Glasgow-Inverclyde-Ayrshire area, caused by bad weather, vandalism and engineering works, and promised a return to standard. The train operator was fined £576,000 under Transport Scotland's tough service quality incentive regime (SQUIRE) for failure to hit targets of cleanliness and graffiti effacement between March 2014 and March 2015. In June 2014 it won a Scottish Award for Business Excellence, and in spring 2015 enjoyed a customer satisfaction rating of 87%, seven points above the UK average, and had been UK Rail Operator of the Year three times in the previous six years.

The Credit Crunch: Rethinkings (and Reopenings)

A National Transport Strategy in 2006 and a Strategic Transport Projects Review in 2008 were both overtaken by the financial collapse and resultant 'credit crunch' beginning in late 2008, which saw the government having to bail out the Royal Bank of Scotland and other financial institutions, inaugurating years of recession, and forcing every organisation to rethink its plans in the light of what was now possible. Fortunately the 30-mile restored Borders Railway to Tweedbank, beyond Galashiels, was already under construction. Its completion on time and within budget (£294 million), in September 2015 marked a high point in the story of renewal that began around 1980. For Transport Scotland challenging issues remain, including the form of the Glasgow Airport rail link and the related question of a north-south 'cross-rail' link in Glasgow itself, using the old City of Glasgow Union line. The DOO (driver-only operation) issue was still very much alive at the end of the second franchise period in 2015, with ScotRail seeking to extend the 'Strathclyde Manning Agreement' beyond the SPT area to the new Bathgate line (opened December 2010), whose trains were designed for driver-only operation, and the RMT Union contesting it as an issue of safety for the travelling public rather than one of jobs or pay levels. Incidentally, with the Bathgate line, Edinburgh and Glasgow were perhaps the only two cities in the world to have four separate railway links.

The Third Franchise

By the time its franchise was up for renegotiation, First ScotRail could point to a generally strong record. New franchises, however, are granted on the case made for future value rather than past achievement. National Express mounted a powerful case to reclaim the contract, fronted by Mary Grant, who had been First ScotRail's managing director in 2004-11. Other bidders included Abellio and Arriva. Evaluation of bids was based 65% on their subsidy requirement and 35% on service quality. Abellio's 7.9% lead on quality was enough to offset its higher subsidy. National Express were runners-up. The Caledonian Sleeper service was made a separate franchise, acquired in May 2014 by the American-owned Serco company for a fifteen-year period, supported by a £100 million investment from the Scottish and UK governments, including £60 million for building of 75 new sleeping cars. Abellio assumed management of ScotRail on 1 April 2015, with Serco taking over the Caledonian Sleepers business a few hours earlier. In July 2017 services into Scotland were also being run by Transpennine Express from Manchester and Liverpool to Glasgow and Edinburgh, by Virgin on the East and West Coast Main Lines, and by Cross Country from Plymouth to Glasgow and Edinburgh, as well as the UK's longest run, Penzance-Aberdeen (785 miles). First Group, having failed to win the franchise, could console itself by having made an anticipatory purchase of vacant time-slots to run its own trains on the East Coast Main Line from 2021: a multiple usage of the track that recalls those earliest days on Scotland's first public railway, more than 200 years before.

Looking Behind, Looking Ahead

In 2015, ScotRail had 4,966 employees, 743 more than in 1994 (Network Rail had a further 2,320 railway workers). It had 347 stations (Network Rail owns Waverley and Glasgow Central), and 1,916 route miles on which 92.7 million passenger journeys had been made in 2014-15, compared with 85.9 million in 2010-11. Its punctuality record was one of the industry's best, with 90.5% of trains arriving within 5 minutes, and 95.9% within 10 minutes, of time. It operated 151 diesel and 144 electric multiple units. In addition it had 100 Mk II coaches, capable of 100 mph running, and two leased Class 68 locomotives. A further 70 Class 385 electric units were on order from Hitachi for introduction from September 2017. In May 2015 the 'ScotRail Alliance' between the train operator and Network Rail was set up, to provide an integrated approach in managing the £2.7 billion renewal programme for the Scottish network in Control Period 5 (2014-19). This included the massive Edinburgh & Glasgow Improvement Project (EGIP) for electrification of the original Edinburgh-Glasgow main line and other improvements. In 2012 its budget was scaled down from the original £1 billion to £650 million, and shorn of some key features, including a connection from the west to the new Edinburgh Gateway station. Full electrification between Waverley and Queen Street was deferred until late 2017 and completion of the entire project is expected to be in 2019. Abellio's franchise is due to end in 2022, with a possible three-year extension. It seemed near

'Uddingston Pride' is the name of the dynamic local group which has adopted Uddingston Station since 2000, and whose floral displays enter the 'Britain in Bloom' competition. (ScotRail)

to premature termination in late 2016, when slipping performance targets, with delays and overcrowding, provoked public anger and an open row involving Abellio, Network Rail and the Scottish Government. In the first half of 2017 things improved, but with engineering work still contributing to delays, ScotRail performance remained a hot political issue at Holyrood. Further extension of the network and improvement of services after 2022 was still a matter for speculation in mid-2017. With the Westminster Department for Transport and the Office of Rail Regulation both having residual responsibilities in Scotland, it was the Holyrood government's policy to press for total accountability for Scottish railways, including infrastructure.

The railways have come a long way from the Kilmarnock & Troon (a route which still survives). We have seen how during the 19th century they became indispensable to economic and social life, though increasingly hampered as they strove to keep pace with change, both by their over-large capital base, with its requirement for regular dividends, and by poorly thought-out curbs imposed by legislation. In the 20th century they not only lost their domination of transport, but endured three upheavals, each followed by years of putting things together again. The first was the Grouping of 1923, of which a joint LMS-LNER statement observed in 1946, "It is a matter of record that the amalgamations under the Railways Act 1921 involved an administrative upheaval which was much more prolonged and disrupting, and far less productive of economies, than was anticipated". The second was Nationalisation in 1948, creating an over-centralised monolith with scant consideration for a radically changing operating environment. Third was privatisation in 1994-97, a hurriedly-confected programme which narrowly avoided disintegration and whose worst effects Scotland has been fortunate to avoid. All three were government-led, with the last two driven by political doctrines deployed for their own sake. Each time, professional railway people (and many civil servants and local authority workers from the 1960s on) have striven to make working sense out of the grand intentions. In one aspect, though, the railways have come full circle. Beginning as an exciting new transport method that would bring riches to its investors, in the 21st century they form a system that can only exist by receiving huge amounts of public subsidy, but still brings riches to its investors. Those in charge of this multi-billion pound system should never forget that it is in place for the travelling public, who are not only its customers, but its stakeholders.

Index

Abellio, 108
Aberlady, 51
Aboyne, 27
Aberdeen, 13, 14, 23, 25, 28, 42, 52, 53,
    58, 63, 70, 71, 85, 88, 89, 93, 104, 107
    Stations: Aberdeen (Joint) 28, 34, 56, 68;
    Guild Street, 27, 28; Kittybrewster, 28;
    Waterloo Quay, 27
Aberdeen Railway, 13, 19, 20f, 25, 27
Accidents: Bellgrove, 101; Calton Tunnel,
69; Castlecary, 73; Hatfield, 104;
Newton, 101; Quintinshill, 61; Tay
Bridge, 36f
Advanced Passenger Train, 98, 105
Airdrie, 33, 85
Alford, 27, 82
Alloa, 41f, 85
Amalgamated Society of Railway
Servants, 37, 48, 58
Annan, 43
Anstruther & St. Andrews Railway, 51
Arbroath, 20, 31, 41
Arbroath & Forfar Railway, 20
Ardrossan, 12, 42, 56, 95, 96
Argyle Line, 95
Arrol, (Sir) William, 40, 47
ASLEF, 69, 96
Aviemore, 50, 62, 90
Ayr, 12, 23, 27, 28, 53, 88, 96, 107
'Ayrshire' Railway, see Glasgow, Paisley,
    Kilmarnock & Ayr
Ayrshire & Wigtownshire Railway, 41

Baird, William & Co., 33, 52
Baker, (Sir) Benjamin, 40, 47
Balerno branch, 66
Ballachulish branch, 56
Ballater, 27
Ballochmyle Viaduct, 21
Balquhidder, 57, 79
Banchory, 23, 71
Banff, 27, 30
Banks, role of, 14
Barrhead, 33, 35, 53
Barry Links, 93
Basic Interval Timetable, 95
Bathgate, 93, 96, 108

Beattock, 4, 19, 98
Beeching, (Lord) Richard, 87, 88f
Beith, 42
Belfast, 23
Berwick, 13, 20, 104
Bilsland, (Lord) Steven, 82, 83
Blair, J.F., 30
Blair Atholl, 97
Bleasdale, Cyril, 101, 102
Bo'ness, 39, 67
Board of Trade, 16, 25, 36, 39, 42, 44, 58, 64
Boddam, 51
Bolton, Sir Ian, 81, 82
Bonar Bridge, 28
Borders Railway, 21, 108
Bouch, (Sir) Thomas, 20, 36f
Brakes on trains, 36, 46
Brechin, 51
British & Irish Grand Junction Railway, 23
British Railways, 80, 83, 86, 100, 101
    Modernisation Plan, 84f, 86, 89;
    'Reshaping', 88; Sectorisation, 94, 95,
    99, 101
British Railways Board (BRB), 88, 92, 95, 96,
    101, 102
British Transport Commission (BTC), 80, 82,
    83, 84, 86, 87, 88
Brown, A.E.H., 82
Buchanan House, 90
Buckie, 52
Burntisland, 18, 20, 31, 51, 60
Burstall, Timothy, 12

Cadder, 84
Cairn Valley Light Railway, 56
Cairnryan, 77
Calder, James, 67, 69
Caledonian Extension Railway, 14
Caledonian Railway, 13, 14, 19, 20, 23, 24, 25,
    26, 27, 28, 29, 30, 32, 33, 34, 39, 40, 47, 51,
    75, 84
Callander & Oban Railway, 30, 38, 40, 56, 92, 104
Cameron, Donald, 83
Cameron, T.F., 81
Campbeltown & Machrihanish Railway, 56, 63
Canals: Forth & Clyde, 34; Union, 34;
    Caledonian, 50

Cardwell, Edward, 25

Carlisle, 13, 19, 20, 24, 28, 35, 47, 68

Carriage Design, 16, 32, 36, 38, 45, 50, 66, 74, 75, 93

Carstairs, 13, 19, 28, 77, 89

Castle, Barbara, 91

Castle Douglas, 23

Castlecary, 73

Catrine, 78

Channel Tunnel, 102, 106

Cheap Trains Act, 42, 43

City of Glasgow Union Railway, 30f, 35, 49, 108

Clydebank, 43, 76

Coatbridge, 106

Colas Rail, 106

'Common Carrier' obligation, 26, 80, 85

Comrie, 51, 76

Concrete, use of, 39

Control system (NBR), 61; (WW2) 78

Cooper, David, 59

Cotton, Peter, 105

Cowlairs Works, 31, 37, 68

Craigellachie, 27

Craigendoran, 49, 77

Crianlarich, 18, 88, 90, 104

Crieff, 51, 57, 79, 85, 104

Cross-Country, 104, 108

Cruden Bay, 51, 53, 62

Cumnock, 21, 23

Cupar, 18, 100

DB (Deutsche Bundesbahn), 105

Dalhousie, Lord, 15, 16

Dalmellington, 23

Dalry, 33, 53

Dalrymple, Lord, 23, 41

Darvel, 57

Deeside Railway, 23, 27, 85

Demurrage dispute, 58

Dickson (later Grant), Mary, 107

Diesel traction, 72, 79, 84, 85, 87, 99,101

Dingwall, 30, 77

Dingwall & Skye Railway, 33, 49, 63

Direct Rail Services, 106

Dollar, 88

Dornoch Light Railway, 56, 92

Dougall, Andrew, 39

Driver-only operation, 97, 108

Drummond, Dugald, 36, 46

Dufftown, 27, 52

Dumbarton, 27, 77, 95, 98

Dumbarton & Balloch Joint Line, 68

Dumfries, 13, 21, 23, 53, 77, 88, 104, 107

Dunblane, 88, 90

Dundee, 12, 14, 20, 31, 34, 41, 47, 57, 76, 82, 85
    Stations: 'Central', 34; East, 41; West, 41; Tay Bridge, 41, 79

Dundee & Arbroath Railway, 32, 41, 68

Dundee & Newtyle Railway, 12

Dundee & Perth & Aberdeen Railway, 27

Dunfermline, 27, 53, 57, 71

East Coast Route, 13, 20, 24, 29, 32, 42, 45, 68, 105, 108

East Coast Trains, 106

Eastfield depot, 24, 85, 105

Edinburgh, 12, 13, 14, 19, 20, 28, 37, 47, 53, 58, 69, 70, 73, 76, 85, 89, 96, 102, 104, 108, 109
    Stations: Canal St, 20; Gateway, 104, 109; General or North Bridge, 20, 29; Haymarket, 13; Lothian Road, 34; Princes Street, 34, 45, 47, 56, 73; Waverley, 29, 34, 73, 75, 79, 82, 101, 109

Edinburgh & Dalkeith Railway, 12

Edinburgh & Glasgow Railway, 12, 19, 20, 25, 27, 30, 31, 32, 34

Edinburgh & Northern Railway, 18

Edinburgh & Perth Railway, 18

Edinburgh Crossrail, 104

Edinburgh, Perth & Dundee Railway, 20, 27, 31

Edzell, 51, 71

EGIP Project, 109

Electrification, 55, 72, 79, 81, 84, 87, 89, 93, 96, 101, 105, 109

Elgin, 23, 24, 30, 42, 51, 52, 66, 85, 90, 107

Elizabethan, 82

Ellis, John, 102, 103

Ellon, 51

Elphinstone, Sir James, 20

English, Welsh & Scottish Railways, 106

Evacuation, 76, 77

Eyemouth, 50, 51

Falkirk, 53

Faslane, 77

Ferguson, William, 42

Fife, 18, 24, 27, 28, 32, 42, 51, 88, 99

First, Second and Third class, 16, 34, 43, 45, 51, 53, 70, 72

First Group/First ScotRail, 105, 107, 108

Flying Scotsman, 70, 72, 81

Forfar, 13, 20, 25, 51, 54, 104

Fort William, 18, 40, 49, 98, 102
Forth & Clyde Junction Railway, 33
Forth Bridge, 29, 37, 40, 42, 47, 51, 62, 67, 76, 102, 103
Fowler, (Sir) John, 30, 40, 47
Fraserburgh, 27, 93
Fraserburgh & St. Combs Light Railway, 56
Freight services, 31, 43, 49, 70, 84f, 86, 87, 89, 90, 91, 92, 94, 99, 106, 107
Freightliner, 89, 91, 99, 106

GB Railfreight, 106
Galashiels, 85
Garnqueen, 20
Gauge of railways, 11, 31, 107
Geddes, Sir Eric, 64, 69
General Terminus & Glasgow Harbour Railway, 19
Georgemas Junction, 44
Gifford & Garvald Light Railway, 56, 71
Girvan, 23, 27
Girvan & Portpatrick Junction Railway, 27, 41
Gladstone, W.E., 15f, 78
Glasgow, 12, 13, 14, 19, 22, 34, 37, 40, 48, 53, 58, 70, 84, 85, 87, 102, 104, 105, 108
    Airport link, 108; North-south link, 19, 30, 108
    Stations: Bridge St, 12, 19, 30, 35, 49; Bridgeton Cross, 51; Buchanan St, 19, 30, 31, 33, 49, 90; Central, 35, 48, 53, 55, 93, 95, 98, 109; College, 30, 49; High St, 49; Hyndland, 48; Queen St, 12, 19, 30, 31, 33, 34, 35, 48, 73, 79, 85, 89, 101; St. Enoch, 30, 35, 45, 53, 55, 72, 82; Singer, 43; South Side, 19, 30, 35, 49; Townhead, 19; Victoria Park, 51
Glasgow & Garnkirk Railway, 19
Glasgow & North Western Railway, 40
Glasgow & South Western Railway, 19, 21, 23, 26, 28, 30, 31, 33, 35, 40, 41, 47, 51, 56, 75
Glasgow and District Transport Committee, 81
Glasgow, Barrhead & Neilston Railway, 18, 19
Glasgow, Bothwell, Hamilton & Coatbridge Railway, 33
Glasgow Central Railway, 48
Glasgow City & District Railway, 48, 72
Glasgow, Dumfries & Carlisle Railway, 14, 19, 23
Glasgow, Paisley, Kilmarnock & Ayr Railway, 12, 13, 19, 21, 22, 23, 33
Glasgow Subway, 48, 63

Glasgow Town Council, 49
Glasgow, Yoker & Clydebank Railway, 48, 51
Gleneagles, 53
Gourock, 89
Granet, Sir Guy, 68
Government and railways, 15, 20, 35f, 42, 45, 48, 49, 60, 61, 64, 74, 76, 84, 86, 91, 92, 96, 102, 104, 110
Grangemouth, 39, 53, 68
Great Glen Pact, 50
Great North Eastern Railway, 104, 105f
Great North of Scotland Railway, 13, 16, 19, 20f, 24, 27f, 31, 42, 46, 51, 52, 55, 57, 75, 83
    Bus services, 57
Great Northern Railway, 40
Greater Glasgow Passenger Transport Authority, 94
Green, Chris, 95, 98, 102
Greenhill, 13, 20
Greenock, 16, 77
Gresley (Sir) Nigel, 73, 74, 75
Gretna, 21, 59, 61, 107
Grouping, 64ff, 74, 79, 83, 110
Guillebaud Inquiry, 86
Gushetfaulds, 18, 85, 106

Hamilton, 53, 57
Hawick, 18, 20, 24
Helensburgh, 27, 33, 85
High Speed Train (HS2), 105
Highland Railway, 13, 23, 28, 33, 39, 40, 46, 50, 52, 57, 75
Hodgson, Richard, 24, 28, 29, 49
Hope-Johnstone, J.J., 14, 20
Horses, 12, 31, 62, 63, 85
Hotels, 53, 81, 91, 99
Hudson, George, 13, 14
Hunterston, 93, 106, 107
Huntly, 24
Hurcomb, (Lord) Cyril, 80, 82, 95

Inchture Tramway, 62
Industrial Relations, 37, 39, 48, 55, 58f, 90, 96, 103
Inglis, Sir Robert, 81
InterCity, 94, 99, 101
Invergarry & Fort Augustus Railway, 50, 71
Invergordon, 62
Inverkeithing, 63
Inverness, 13, 16, 18, 23, 24, 40, 50, 51, 52, 53, 63, 65, 68, 70, 85, 90, 98, 104, 107

Inverness & Aberdeen Junction Railway, 24, 28
Inverness & Nairn Railway, 53
Inverness & Perth Junction Railway, 27, 28
Inverurie, 55, 69, 98

Jedburgh, 81
Jellicoe Specials, 63
Johnston, Tom, 72
Johnstone, 53
Jones, David, 66, 72

Keith, 24, 27, 52, 62
Kelso, 81, 84
Killin, 38, 83
Kilmacolm, 96
Kilmarnock, 11, 13, 31, 33, 35, 53, 68, 85, 97,
    107
Kilmarnock & Troon Railway, 11, 17, 110
Kilwinning, 42
Kincardine, 57, 71
Kinnaber Junction, 41, 66
Kinross, 18, 47, 92
Kirkcaldy, 42, 53
Kittybrewster, 31
Knapp, Jimmy, 97
Kyle of Lochalsh, 30, 49, 50, 53, 63, 88, 95, 98

Ladybank, 92
Lanarkshire & Ayrshire Railway, 42, 56
Lanarkshire & Dumbartonshire Railway, 52, 55
Larbert, 37
Lauder Light Railway, 56
Leadbetter, John, 13f
Learmonth, John, 13, 18, 21, 51
Leith, 34, 56
Lesmahagow, 25
Leven & East Fife Railway, 33, 51
Light Railways, 56
Liverpool, 12, 108
Lloyd George, David, 58
Lochaber, 49, 77
Lockerbie, 13, 104
Locomotive Design, 31, 32, 46, 66, 73, 74f, 83, 85
Locomotive Works, 31, 55, 68, 88
London, 12, 20, 34, 42, 70, 72, 82, 85, 89, 95,
    98, 102, 104, 105
London & North Eastern Railway, 64, 67ff,
    79, 91
London & North Western Railway, 20, 28, 40
London Midland & Scottish Railway, 64, 67ff,
    70, 91

Lossiemouth, 23
MacBrayne, David & Co., 68
McCall, James, 13, 21
McCulloch, John R., 15
Macduff, 27, 82
MacGregor, John, 101
McIntosh, J.F., 66
'MacPuff', 88
Mail services, see Post Office
Mallaig, 18, 49, 50, 98
Marples, Ernest, 87
Matheson, Alexander, 13
Matheson, Donald, 55, 61, 67
Matthews, Sir Ronald, 74, 79f
Maybole, 23, 27
Merry-go-round trains, 89
Methil, 51
Mid Calder, 29
Midland Railway, 28, 35, 39, 45, 47, 68
Miller, James, 55
Miller, John, 21
Millerhill, 89
Ministry of (later Department for) Transport,
    64, 65, 74, 80, 82, 88, 92, 95, 96, 105, 110
Mixed Trains, 46
Moffatt, William, 42
Monkland & Kirkintilloch Railway, 12
Monklands Railways, 26, 27
Montgomery, Steve, 107f
Montrose, 41, 93
Morayshire Railway, 19, 23
Morrison, James, 16
Mossend, 84, 106, 107
Motherwell, 25, 48, 53, 95
Motorail, 85
Muirkirk, 28, 104

Nairn, 24
National Express, 103, 104f, 108
National factories, 62
National Union of Railwaymen, 69, 97, 103
National Wages Board, 71
Nationalisation, 16, 59f, 64, 78f, 80, 110
Ness, James, 82, 85, 90
Network Rail, 4, 104, 105, 108, 109
Newburgh & North Fife Railway, 58
Newlands, Alexander, 69
Newton Stewart, 33
Nightrider train, 95
North Berwick, 95, 101
North British Locomotive Co., 66, 69, 85

North British Railway, 13, 14, 18, 19, 20, 21, 23, 24, 27, 28, 29, 31, 33, 34, 35, 36, 39, 40, 46, 47, 51, 55, 61, 65, 75, 84
North Eastern Railway, 47, 64
North Queensferry, 18
'Northern Belle', 72

Oban, 30, 40, 57, 95
Office of Passenger Rail Franchising, 102, 104
Office of Rail Regulation/Rail and Road, 102, 110
Old Meldrum, 27
Operation Phoenix, 98
Orr, (Sir) Andrew, 23, 28

Paisley, 16, 53, 56, 85
    Stations: Canal, 96, 101; Gilmour St, 19
Paisley & Renfrew Railway, 31
Parker, Sir Peter, 94, 95
Parliament (Edinburgh), 105
Parliament (Westminster), 16, 19, 25, 27, 47, 48
Parliamentary Trains, 16, 42, 43
Passenger Facilities, 34, 38, 45, 53, 74
Passenger Focus Scotland, 107
Passenger service closures, 62, 71, 82, 83, 88f
Passenger Tax, 16
Passenger Transport Partnerships, 107
Pendolinos, 4, 105
Perth, 13, 20, 23, 25, 26, 28, 31, 33, 41, 47, 53, 57, 68, 78, 85, 89, 91, 92, 107
Peterhead, 27, 51, 93
Polloc & Govan Railway, 19
Portland, Duke of, 57
Portpatrick Railway, 23f, 26f, 40
Portpatrick & Wigtownshire Joint Railway, 40
Portsoy, 42, 52
Post Office, 23f, 25, 28, 40, 99
Prince's Dock, 55, 68
Princess Victoria, 83
Privatisation, 99, 101, 110
Provincial Services, 94
Pullman cars, 45

RMT Union, 103, 108
Races to the North, 41, 42, 66
Radio control, 98
Railtrack, 101, 102, 103, 104, 106
Railway & Canal Commission, 36, 58
Railway & Canal Traffic Acts: 1854, 25, 85; 1888, 44; 1894, 44, 59; 1913, 59
Railway Clearing House, 22, 29

Railway Companies' Association, 43, 60
Railway Executive (World War I), 61, 65
Railway Executive (BR), 80f, 81
'Railway Mania', 18ff, 23
Railway Rates Tribunal, 65, 70, 73
Railways Act 1921, 65, 69, 70, 74, 76
Rates and Charges, 43f, 63, 68, 70
Ravenscraig Steelworks, 93, 106
Regional Railways, 101, 102
Regulation of Railways Acts: 1844, 16; 1868, 34, 1889, 46; 48, 61, 64
Reid, Sir Bob (I), 94, 95, 100
Reid, Sir Bob (II), 100
Renfrew, 53
Renshaw, Sir Charles Bine, 59
'Reshaping of British Railways', 88
Riccarton Junction, 82
Rifkind, Sir Malcolm, 101
Road competition, 52f, 69, 70, 72, 73, 74, 84, 85, 95, 103
Robertson, Sir Brian, 82, 86, 87, 95
Rosyth, 63
Rothesay Dock, 55
Royal Commission on Railways:1865-7, 29; 1911, 59
Royal Scot, 70, 72
Royden, (Lord) Thomas, 77
Rutherglen, 30

SMT Co., 70
St. Andrews, 91
St. Margaret's Works, 31
St. Rollox Works, 31, 37, 68, 98
Salkeld, Thomas, 25, 28
Sanquhar, 23, 103
ScotRail, 25, 95, 96, 97, 99, 100, 102, 103, 104, 109
'ScotRail Alliance', 109
Scottish Central Railway, 13, 20, 26, 27
Scottish Executive, later Government, 107, 109f
Scottish Midland Junction Railway, 13, 20, 25, 26
Scottish North Eastern Railway, 25, 27
Scottish Railway Stockholders Association, 73
Scottish Region (British Railways), 81, 82, 87, 89, 91, 94, 96, 97, 98, 99
    Area Board, 82, 88, 90; 'Highland Lines, 90; Two-tier management, 90, 93, 95
Scottish Waggon Owners' Association, 54
Serco, 108
Serpell Report, 96
Shareholders, 12, 16, 18, 21, 23, 25, 27, 29, 37, 39, 47, 49, 64, 70f, 72f, 74, 78, 79, 80

Shipping services, 30, 62, 66, 83, 91, 94
Silloth, 24
Sleeping cars and services, 45, 70, 85, 98, 102, 108
'Social Railway' concept, 91
Solway Junction Railway, 29, 71
Solway Viaduct, 29
SQUIRE regime, 108
Stagecoach, 103, 106
Stair, see Dalrymple
Stamp, (Lord) Josiah, 68, 71, 72, 74, 75, 77
Stanier, Sir W.A., 75
Starlight Specials, 82
Stedeford Committee, 87
Stephenson, George, 11, 12
Stevenson, Robert, 12
Stirling, 13, 27, 33, 47, 53, 85, 104
Stirling, John, 33f
Stock Exchanges, 14
Stocks and Shares, 25, 28, 60, 79f
Stranraer, 27, 40, 77, 88, 104
Strategic Rail Authority, 104, 107
Strathaven, 57
Strathclyde Manning Agreement, 97, 108
Strathclyde PTA and PTE, 94, 95, 96, 100, 101, 103, 107
Strathclyde Region, 94, 103
Strathearn, 57, 79
Strathmore, 12, 20, 82
Strathspey Railway, 27
Strikes, 39, 48, 64, 69, 90, 96, 97, 103
Subsidies, 49, 74, 91, 94, 110
Sutherland, (third) Duke of, 28, 33

Tay Bridge, 34, 36f, 40, 41, 58
Telegraphs, 25, 29
Titchfield, Marquess of, 11
Thompson, (Sir) Matthew, 40, 47
Thompson, (Sir) James, 39
Thompson, Edward, 75
Thornton, 85, 89
Thorpe, W.G., 90, 91
Thurso, 28, 29, 33, 63, 77, 86, 88, 98
TOPS, 93

Traders' Wagons, 31, 54, 61
Train Ferries, 20
Transpennine Express, 108
Transport Act: 1947, 79; 1953, 81, 85; 1962, 88; 1968, 91
Transport Scotland, 106, 107, 108
Transport Tribunal, 85
Transport Users' Consultative Committee, 82f
Troon, 11, 57
Turnberry, 53
Tweedbank, 108
Tweeddale, Lord, 49

Uddingston, 109

Virgin Railways, 104, 105, 106, 108

Wages and working conditions, 37, 38, 39, 48, 63, 64, 69, 71, 78, 84, 86, 90, 96, 108
Wagon pooling, 58, 61, 71
Wagonways, 11
Walker, John, 39
Wanlockhead, 71
Waverley Route, 29, 81, 88
Wedgwood, Sir Ralph, 72
Weir, Lord, 72
Wemyss & Buckhaven Railway, 51
Wemyss Bay, 36, 89
Wemyss, Randolph, 51
West Coast Route, 13, 20, 24, 29, 42, 68, 93, 96, 105, 106, 107
West Coast Trains, 104
West Highland Railway, 49, 50, 75, 77, 92, 98
Whiteinch Railway, 48
Whitelaw, William, 52, 68, 69, 70, 72, 74, 78
Whithorn, 33, 82
Wick, 28, 29, 33, 62, 75, 78, 88, 98
Wick & Lybster Light Railway, 56, 78
Wigtownshire Railway, 33, 40
Windmillcroft Dock, 19
Wishaw, 53
Women workers, 62, 63, 78, 106
Workmen's trains, 42f